THAT GOD'S WORK BE DISPLAYED

THAT GOD'S WORK BE DISPLAYED

What I Saw After I Lost My Sight

by John H. Erickson

Edited and prepared for publication by Jessica Royer Ocken
Oak Park, IL

Book design by Mona Luan

Cover concept by JP Erickson and Ellie Erickson

© John H. Erickson

All rights reserved.

No part of this book may be reproduced in any form, including transmitting, or by any electronic or mechanical means, including informational storage and retrieval systems, without permission in writing from the author, except by a reviewer, who may quote brief passages in a review.

December 2013, First Printing

CONTENTS

A Note from the Author	1

BEING A KID   **3**
Growing Up in Mayberry	5
Bud and the Babe	7
Right and Wrong	11
Sports and "The Catch"	16
The Cottage in Michigan	20
The Beginning of Faith	24
The Beginning of Loss	29
The Real Diagnosis	32
Coming Home	38
Getting By	41
What I Had Never Seen Before	45
Learning A New Language	49

HIGH SCHOOL   **53**
Introduction to OPRF	55
My Dean For Life	57
The Teacher Who Knew the Ropes	63
The Three Amigos	68

My Best New Friend in High School Was Blond	72
Last Rites at 16	76
Rebuilding Time For Big John	80
Part Two of My Spiritual Journey	87
My Return to Sports	89
Getting Into the Dating Game	96
High School Finale	102

COLLEGE & BEYOND — 105

Here Come The Irish!	107
A New Friend	114
Moving Forward	121
Graduate School	123
On the Dance Floor	127
Another New Friend	130

ADULTHOOD — 135

Breaking Into the Real World of Work	137
The "Muni Go-For"	141
Step Three of My Spiritual Journey	145
The Dating Life	153

A New Best Friend,
    For the Rest of My Life   159
Family Man   169
Growing Older   178

Epilogue   *183*

A NOTE FROM THE AUTHOR

My name is John Erickson, and I am a very happily married man. My wife Jane and I are proud parents of two great kids: our son, JP, and our daughter, Ellie.

I make my living as a registered investment advisor in Chicago. I love to sail on Lake Michigan during the summer, downhill ski in Utah in the winter, and build model tanks all year round.

I also like to bungee jump, rappel down the sides of hotels in downtown Chicago, and climb up the stairs inside other high rises like the John Hancock Building. I've taken trapeze lessons with my son, JP, and I've driven a 60-ton British tank over a Lincoln Continental!

I also happen to be legally blind. I have been since the age of 12. I have a visual acuity of about 20/1000, rather than 20/20. And I need hearing aids due to serious hearing loss in recent years.

In one of my favorite movies, *It's a Wonderful Life*, Clarence the Angel says, "Funny, isn't it, George? Each man's life touches so many others."

I really like that line, but this is more a book about the people who have touched my life than it is about my life in particular.

As I look back over the years, I can see how so many of the people I encountered embodied God's love and were part of His work in my life.

Along my life's journey, I have slowly come to understand what Jesus Christ has done for me, and how much He loves me. It took the loss of my sight to see it clearly.

BEING A KID

GROWING UP IN MAYBERRY

One of the first and most favorite record albums I ever heard was Bill Cosby's *I Started Out As a Child*. In it he tells the story of his childhood, full of great friends and family. My life started out much the same way.

My earliest memories are those of a safe, comfortable home in River Forest, Illinois—a small, relatively affluent suburb of Chicago. River Forest had a population of 12,000 people 50 years ago, and it's got 11,000 people now. This is not the result of people abandoning the village, but rather it's the result of people coming back to where they grew up, buying the older, smaller homes, and tearing them down to build larger ones. The village is full of people who grew up here a generation ago and have returned to bring up their own families.

It could be said that people from River Forest are a lot like salmon: they are born here, they leave to go to school and get a job, but they eventually come right back here to breed.

I am one of those salmon.

When I was growing up, it was truly the kind of place where Andy, Opie, and Aunt Bee would have felt right at home.

My family's first house was a cool tri-level home with three small bedrooms and a half-basement. I shared one of those bedrooms with my twin brother and best friend, Pete. When our two younger sisters, Karen and JoAnne, came along, they shared the other small bedroom, and my folks had their own bedroom on the third level.

BUD AND THE BABE

When it comes to my mom and dad, Joan Carroll Erickson (known throughout her life as "the Babe") and Hubbard H. Erickson Jr. (who was known as "Bud"), I hit the proverbial Parent Jackpot. I can see today that God used them to shape me into who I am, and to show me the depth of His love.

Both my mom and dad were born in River Forest and lived most of their lives there. They attended Oak Park-River Forest High School in the 1940s.

My dad was 15 years old when Pearl Harbor was bombed and the United States entered World War II. As with many young men of that generation, going into the service right from high school was a no-brainer for my dad. As he tells it, he was not a very good student, and he might never have gotten out of high school if not for the war! My dad would tell us this whenever he wanted to commend us for good grades or console us when we were upset about getting a not-so-good grade.

My father enlisted in the Navy when he turned 17. Because of his love of flying, he went into aviation where he eventually won his wings and was commissioned as a naval aviator. By the end of the war he had decided to make the Navy his career. Unfortunately, shortly thereafter my grandfather became seriously ill, and financial pressures forced my dad to leave active duty after 4 years. He transferred to a naval reserve squadron so he could continue to fly on weekends and come home to work with his father during the week to produce the Chicago National Boat Show, which my grandfather had founded in the early 1930s. After the boating industry came together to form a national trade association, which took over the show, my grandfather was able to retire and close his office.

For the next several years of my dad's working life, he and his partner managed the physical operations for many of the major trade shows and expositions using Navy Pier in downtown Chicago. Navy Pier at that time was nothing more than a warehouse, which had been abandoned by the Navy following the war, and my father actually had to live there in a converted office—often for weeks at a time—during major events. As the rapidly growing post-war trade show and convention industry began to blossom, my father went on to produce major industry events of his own at the request of some of the newly established trade associations, first in Chicago, then all over the United States, and eventually even overseas. He's now recognized as one of the founding fathers of the post-war trade show and convention industry in the United States.

My mom graduated from high school after WWII was over, and she went on to Marymount College in New York and got her teaching degree. She was teaching grade school in Oak Park when her cousin called to invite her to go bowling. Her cousin then called my dad and asked him to join them. My dad thought the other person coming along was just another guy, so he was very pleasantly surprised when the additional bowler turned out to be my mom.

They got married in August of 1955 and were living in a small River Forest apartment when they unexpectedly became the parents of twins, my brother Pete and me, the very next June. (The twins were the surprise, not becoming parents!) My sister Karen was born less than two years later in April 1958, so my folks had the dubious distinction of having two children on their first anniversary, two children on their second, three children on their third anniversary, and finally having more years married than children on their fourth anniversary.

My mom retired from teaching just before Pete and I were born, and she was able to be a stay at home mom for all of us. In that role she always found time to be whatever was needed at our grade school: Cub Scout den mother, Girl Scout leader, picture lady, room mother, and PTA member. At the same time, my dad always found the time to be a Cub Scout leader when needed, and either a coach or manager of Pete's or my Little League team.

But I'm getting ahead of myself!

RIGHT AND WRONG

There's little doubt in my mind that my very first understanding of the world around me and my early definitions of right and wrong were formed as a toddler—the time when just about all communications between child and adult are dominated by "No!" My parents have told me several times that Pete and I were very active as infants, always playing off one another—in both good and bad ways. A typical example of this behavior was captured on film one day as Pete and I ate our lunch in our highchairs at my grandmother's house. Pete is looking right at the camera and putting a piece of food in his mouth. I'm sitting next to him, reaching over to his tray and taking food off his plate! My mother says Pete and I generally played well together, and she really didn't know at the time how full her hands were with us because we were her first.

Luckily for Pete and me, our dad was not quick to anger, nor was he a "yeller." He was, however, quick to pull us aside and in a very slow and deliberate tone—bordering on menacing—remind us of what was appropriate and inappropriate behavior. I'm sure this started when Pete and I were as young as three years old. Very slowly, as the lessons of appropriate behavior became clear to me, two basic precepts came into focus: good behavior is rewarded, and bad behavior leads to correction and sometimes punishment. I caught on to this pretty quickly.

As a preschooler, I had a great interest in the garbage men coming each week. During the nice-weather months, I made it a point to go out and see the garbage men come to our house in their big truck. I loved to watch them pour the garbage into the back of the truck and then see the powerful crusher devour it. My parents say the garbage men were the only ones to whom I would ultimately surrender the tattered remains of my baby blanket or "nonny," as baby blankets were called in my home.

I suspect it was because of this interest that when Pete and I were about six, Dad took us out to the military museum at Cantigny in Winfield, Illinois. As long as I was so interested in heavy metal vehicles, I might as well know about the military as a career, along with sanitary engineering. Well, once I saw my first tank, garbage trucks were an interest of the past.

Not long after that, my father showed Pete and me how to build model planes and tanks. I was hooked. There was a short lapse in my model-building career during the years when I first began losing my sight. However, when that time was over and my eyesight stabilized, I learned to build and paint my models with a closed-circuit TV enlarger. More about that later, but suffice to say I haven't stopped building models since.

❧ ❧ ❧ ❧

Next it was time to leave home for a bit and experience school. It became clear to me very quickly that the same rules applied at school as at home: good behavior is rewarded, and bad behavior is not. My first memory of getting punished at school was being sent to the Time Out rug in Kindergarten for chasing another little boy around the room with a block I was pretending was a gun. Unfortunately, my interest in guns was not shared and rewarded by most of my early educators.

Nonetheless, I believe society as a whole was far safer for many years as a result of my sentence to the Time Out rug. This nip-it-in-the-bud action left me with a lasting message: not everyone shares my enthusiasm for military hardware and history. Still, the military and war were hugely fascinating to me. Those interests were a driving force throughout grade school. My daughter was really interested one day to find old report cards of mine from second grade where the teacher said, "John is very artistic but focuses only on drawing tanks and ships." The military remains an interest and hobby of mine today.

The grade school my siblings and I attended, Washington School, was just two and a half blocks away, on the other side of our block, and we did not have to cross a single busy street to get there. We walked to class, and it was a chapter right out of the *Leave it to*

Beaver TV show. Pete and I were good students and got basically identical grades—except that Pete always got an A in handwriting and I got a B, which I realize was an absolute gift, in retrospect. Although I loved to draw tanks and planes, writing was just about getting my ideas down on paper. How it looked wasn't important to me at all. My handwriting grade should have been a C—or worse!

Our good grades also put Pete and me in good standing with our parents and grandparents. Both sets of my grandparents also lived in River Forest, less than one mile away from our house. Grampa Joe Carroll, my maternal grandfather, was such an outspoken supporter of good grades that he would often offer 25 cents for every A we got on a report card. This might not seem like much now, but at the time, Pete and I were getting 25 cents a week in allowance for doing our light chores around the house like taking out the trash and keeping our room picked up. The prospect of getting a month or two of allowance for working a little harder to get As was well worth the effort!

SPORTS AND "THE CATCH"

But more important to both of us than school work was being pretty good in gym class and other athletics. In those first years of grade school, I was one of the taller boys in the class, and Pete was a couple inches shorter than me. In general, I was respectable in all sports, but Pete was a little faster, quicker, and more talented.

We were the offensive ends of the Washington grade school football team, and at the pinnacle of our football career there was an end-around-with-a-pass play where Pete successfully took the handoff from the running back and passed the football to me for a touchdown. My height helped me in basketball and volleyball, but kickball was my forte. I had a knack for punting the ball with great distance and accuracy, and I actually posted home runs while playing kickball inside the gym—one time by kicking the ball through the opposite basketball hoop, once by kicking it out the window of the gym, and a third time by wedging the ball between the roof and the rafters!

During the summers back in the 1960s, the only non-school sports program around in River Forest was Little League. It was for boys 7 to 12 years old and ran for about ten weeks. It was a great opportunity to become teammates with boys from other grade schools. I have great memories of playing Little League, and even a handful of memories of stellar performances on the field.

Not long ago, following a high school reunion, I was getting a ride home with Joe Barrett. Joe was not only a classmate from high school, but had been one of the best baseball players in Little League during the years when Pete and I played. I was utterly amazed when Joe suddenly asked me if I remembered "that amazing catch" in the outfield I made one time when he was batting.

I was delighted to tell him I did remember

that catch, but I had to share my perspective on the event. When Joe had come to the plate, everyone on our team had dropped back, including me in right field. We expected the ball to be hit sharply. A pitch or two later, Joe's bat cracked, and he sent a screaming line drive right toward me in right field. When he first hit the ball, I took a couple steps backward, fearing the worst, but then I saw that the ball was not going high into the air, so I started to charge, now fearing it would drop in front of me. But after a few steps forward, I realized the ball was about to careen over my head, so I shot up my glove hand in sheer desperation! By the grace of God, I caught the ball and was so surprised at what had happened that I wasn't quite sure what to do next, at least for a split second or two. Apparently, fans saw the play as a fine defensive reaction in the outfield rather than, as I saw it, a close call and near humiliation of epic proportions!

Pete and I wrapped up our Little League careers in the summer between sixth and seventh grade, but that wasn't the only activity we enjoyed together. Our dad always made sure there were plenty of things for us to do at home. When he wasn't working at his office, Dad was working around the house—mowing the lawn in the summer or building an ice skating rink in the backyard during the winter. This was so cool to us because not only could we skate there, but lots of kids from our neighborhood came to our house to skate too! Dad managed this while running his own company and flying around the country to produce trade shows and conventions.

THE COTTAGE IN MICHIGAN

Because he had his own business, Dad realized very early in his marriage that there weren't going to be two- or three-week family vacations because he had to be available at the office all year round. So he bought some wooded property in Michigan on the shore of Lake Michigan, just over two hours away from our home, where we would vacation almost every weekend during the summer after Little League was done. We camped out there for the first time the summer when Pete and I were six, Karen was four, and our sister JoAnne was just an infant, having been born that very summer of 1962. (My parents were very brave to camp with so many small children.) Dad built a very simple but adequate and functional cottage there the next summer, and he worked each weekend we were there to slowly improve it, summer after summer.

Occasionally, this meant Pete and I were called upon to help with things like moving railroad ties or piles of sand and dirt from here to there, or our favorite: crawling under the house to turn the water on and off. In between these occasional chores, there were days and days of playing on the beach, in the water, and my favorite: Pete and I hunting each other down in the woods with our toy machine guns!

And there was another reason we all enjoyed going to the cottage in Michigan: the Kettlehut family. Just a year or two after we started vacationing there, a childhood friend of my mom's, Bill Kettlehut, bought property down the beach from our cottage, and the Kettlehut family began making regular trips to Michigan just like us. There were also four children in their family: Billy, Susan, Betsy, and Nancy. Susan was a year older than Pete and me, while Betsy was a year younger. Billy was three years older, and Nancy was three years younger.

When Pete and I were about 9, I think, we still regularly enjoyed playing army in the woods. But soon after that we realized there were really cute girls just down the beach—and they were wearing swimming suits! After that, doing just about anything with the Kettlehuts was more fun than playing army!

And we couldn't keep them a secret from our other friends for long. Whereas friends used to say, "Yes, sure!" when we asked them to come to the cottage for a weekend with us, they now started to say, "Well, will the Kettlehuts be up there too?"

Seeing Susan, Betsy, Bill, and Nancy almost every time we went to the cottage became a regular part of our time there. The Kettlehuts taught us all how to waterski when Billy was old enough to drive the motorboat, and Pete and I always called Susan, Betsy, and Nancy when we collected firewood to have a fire on the beach, which was almost every weekend. They always brought graham crackers, chocolate bars, and marshmallows to make the S'mores.

For our tenth birthday, Pete and I received a ten-foot Styrofoam sail boat called The Snark. (Note: Getting joint or shared gifts for birthdays is a definite risk of being a twin.) Dad taught the two of us the fundamentals of sailing on Lake Michigan. Even though he added a fiberglass coating to the hull of the boat, the rigors of having two boys crashing it in the surf resulted in The Snark cracking in half two years later.

By that time, sailing had become one of our favorite things to do, so with the help of our parents, Pete and I bought a 12-foot Sunfish to replace The Snark. That was the summer we both turned 12.

My memories of being at the cottage in Michigan are some of the best of my whole life. When I visit there today, it is the greatest example of the beauty of God's creation I know. Although I can't see the details of the woods, the water, and the sunsets anymore, I can hear the waves on the beach, feel the sun and the wind, and I have the memories of God's countless blessings of my years there.

THE BEGINNING OF FAITH

About the same time as Pete and I started school, we started going to church and Sunday School as well. My family regularly attended St. Luke's Catholic Church in River Forest, and we all grew up with regular prayers at meals and bedtime. I found the precepts and teachings of the church in perfect harmony with both school and home life. Namely, God also rewarded good behavior, most of the time, and He quite often punished bad behavior, although mostly in the stories of the Old Testament. My earliest evaluations of Jesus were that He either decided Himself (or was coerced by God the Father) to come to Earth and teach us all the things the prophets had failed to explain well, and eventually He died on the cross to offset what the nuns called "original sin." Original sin guaranteed that none of us humans could be perfect and slide easily into heaven, regardless of how good our actions were here on earth.

So, as I figured it, Jesus had to come to Earth and die on the cross so we could get past original sin and be judged by God on the merits of our own lives. I knew I wasn't alone in this belief, either. In one of my favorite songs as a kid, the Everly Brothers' "Last Kiss," the singer lamented the loss of his "baby" and pledged to be good so he could see her again in heaven someday. To me, the church offered a very clear framework of dos and don'ts that I could use as guidelines in my life. The one unsettling thing that occurred quite often, though, was that I would see others clearly violate these rules and regulations, and they would not only get away with it, but the powers that be would not even seem to care. Still, I stuck with the rules and regulations anyway. This was perhaps because I was a better follower than rebel and independent thinker during the early years of grade school.

For many years, the integration of these three worlds—home life, school, and church—

was seamless and easy. However, as I grew older, heard more Scripture at church, and became familiar with more and more passages, inconsistencies started to pop up. There were passages in the Bible that did not back up my beliefs that God rewarded good behavior and punished bad.

The stories I remember being the most puzzling were the parable of the prodigal son, the workers in the field, and the stewards and the talents. They just did not seem fair.

In the parable of the prodigal son (Luke 15:11-32), one son is obedient to his father, while the other acts like a selfish, self-centered, ungrateful brat and asks his father to give him the inheritance that will someday be coming to him. Then the son takes off and squanders the money. When he has nothing and is suffering much, he comes to his senses and realizes what a jerk he's been. He decides to return to his home and ask his father if he can work for him. When he gets there, his father sees him coming and runs to greet him. Then the father orders that a party be thrown in the son's honor.

Seeing all this happen, the other son, who has always been obedient to his father, is justifiably upset with the whole event. He says to the father, "Hey, what gives? I've worked hard for you and done everything you've asked, not like this brother of mine, and you've never thrown a party for me!" The father tells the son not to worry about it. That he will reward him someday, but for now everyone should rejoice because the other son was lost but has returned to them.

Scripture never says anything more about how the good son took that explanation, but it always seemed lame to me. It clearly did not fit into my fundamental beliefs about being rewarded for good behavior and not rewarded for bad.

Those other two parables did not show much fairness (as I understood it) either. In the parable of the workers in the field (Matthew 20:1-16), the owner of the field hires workers throughout the day, but pays them all exactly the same amount when the day is over. In the parable of the talents, (Matthew 25:14-30) the wealthy master gives each of three stewards different amounts of money and gets mad at the one who received the smallest amount because he did not invest it wisely.

Luckily, I was able to put the cognitive dissonance these stories created aside by deciding they must be one of those mysteries that humans aren't supposed to understand.

THE BEGINNING OF LOSS

Halfway through fifth grade, we moved to a bigger house in River Forest. This meant a new grade school for one year, which was a whopping four blocks away and still did not require the crossing of a single busy street to get there. The next year it was time to move on to River Forest Junior High. This was a momentous progression in our lives, but the junior high stood adjacent to the new grade school, so travel plans were same as before.

Junior high brought on a lot of changes, and most of them were not good. The most noticeable and important to me at that time was that I lost my rather high physical status versus my fellow male peers. Despite wearing glasses for mild near-sightedness, I had enjoyed quite a bit of status and popularity in elementary school, probably due to being "one of the twins" and one of the tallest kids in the class. Pete and I had many times been elected squad leaders in gym class, which was a big deal to me.

But when seventh grade rolled around, within what seemed like a matter of months, other boys morphed into superior specimens of male adolescence. In contrast, during that first semester of seventh grade, I noticed a significant decline in my athletic performance. When playing football that fall, I no longer dominated other players. I felt my performance decline to below average, which was very disheartening.

And maybe even more troubling to me, I no longer felt I was pleasing the gym teachers with my performance. One time in early seventh grade, I was trying to put a positive spin on my now average physique by mentioning how light I was to my new gym teacher. He replied, "Well, muscle weighs more than fat." I don't think I was oversensitive to take that as a cut.

At the same time, I also seemed to slip from the higher scholastic tier I had enjoyed throughout grade school. My seventh grade grades fell from mostly As and an occasional

B to Bs and Cs. I found each class far more challenging than any I had experienced before. I did not complain to my folks about most of these things because they seemed in no position to solve my problems. If my grades were falling, I had to work harder. If I was no longer a good athlete, maybe my time of such glory was just over, and I had to come to grips with that.

I'd always thought of myself as having a healthy childhood, as I hadn't experienced any unusual maladies (other than falling off a fence and running into a TV set while racing through the house with Pete, both of us requiring some stitches in the head). But my folks took me to the family doctor one day to check out my complaint of headaches. During that visit, I remember mentioning not just the headaches but also the advent of "mobility problems," as I think I called them because calling it "weird clumsiness" didn't seem very medical. My doctor chalked up my complaints to the stress of junior high—a very reasonable diagnosis at the time, as I saw it.

The Beginning of Loss   31

THE REAL DIAGNOSIS

Early during the second semester of seventh grade, I suddenly noticed that the words on the chalkboard were very blurry. If I removed my glasses, the words were clearer for a few moments, but my eyes would soon start to hurt. Presuming that a new prescription for my glasses was in order, we scheduled the next available appointment with the eye doctor. During his initial examination, he was very concerned to find that I had lost 25% of my vision in one eye and 40% in the other. He did not have an explanation for such a loss and recommended that my parents take me over to the local hospital to determine the nature of the problem.

I was not really alarmed at the prospect of going to the hospital for further testing because the hospital had always done a good job of patching me up after mishaps. After all, I wasn't a kid anymore. I was 12 and a half—practically a teenager!

So I checked into the local hospital, but after a week of tests, nothing showed a clear diagnosis. However, they suspected that some kind of pressure around my optic nerve was responsible for the loss of sight, and probably the other maladies too. So we next went to Illinois Masonic Medical Center—a bigger hospital in downtown Chicago that was known for having experts with experience in neurology. It was there that Dr. Ronald Pawl came into my life. Dr. Pawl was a neurosurgeon at Masonic and would become the man who literally saved my life nine times in the next three years. And Dr. Pawl had a great bedside manner. Like my Dad, he spoke with confidence and authority, and I found it easy to put my trust in him.

The routine at Masonic seemed much the same as it had been at our local hospital: I spent my day in a nice, comfortable bed and got to order my meals a whole day at a time. I thought the food was quite good, actually, so at first I did not mind the regular trips out of the room for this test or that, because I assumed it was just a matter of time before they figured out what was wrong and took measures to fix everything. However, rather quickly, these tests became more and more invasive and challenging. The most painful was a spinal tap, where fluid is removed from your spine with a pretty bad looking needle. But I kept thinking it was just a matter of time until they fixed everything.

I don't remember anyone talking to me about the doctors' final diagnosis, but I know now that they decided I was suffering from aqueductal stenosis. Everyone's brain produces cerebral fluid, and that fluid regularly drains from the head into the chest cavity, where it is reabsorbed into the body. For some reason (which was never determined), my fluid had stopped draining, and the subsequent pressure it produced had manifested itself first with headaches, then with mobility problems, and finally with loss of vision as my optic nerves were damaged. The spinal taps had provided the conclusive evidence that such pressure existed. The treatment was to be implanting a small plastic tube called a shunt to act as a bypass around the damaged drainage ventricle.

So, one morning I left my hospital room for what I thought was one more test, but instead was a surgery to put the shunt in. I woke up many hours later in the intensive care unit. I was very weak, and there were all kinds of tubes going in and out of my body. There was also a lot of discomfort on the right side of my head and neck, and all my hair had been shaved off! My eyesight was a lot worse than it had been before. I could tell there were hospital people walking around, but I couldn't see who they were.

Sometime later, I was moved to my own hospital room, and my folks were there. That was a huge comfort. They explained the operation to me and said I had to rest until it was time to go home. I don't remember anyone specifically telling me a prognosis of what was to come, but I had lots of time to think about it the next several days.

I did a lot of thinking because there wasn't much else I could do. I could hear the TV, but I could no longer see the screen. Words on paper were now too blurry to read, so there were no comic books or *Mad* magazines. I couldn't even draw, which had been one of my favorite pastimes, because I couldn't see a pencil line on paper.

All of these realizations made me think about the fun of summer and sports. Baseball, basketball, and volleyball would be impossible with my new level of sight. Kickball, my favorite, was out too. I thought I could probably still kick the ball, but how would I run to the bases if I couldn't see them? And then, of course, there was school to think about. What was I going to do about reading all those books? How would I take notes in class if I couldn't see the blackboard? How would I take notes if I couldn't see the lines on the notebook paper? I didn't like feeling so helpless. I felt powerless, as though all my talents and abilities had been sucked out of me.

But one thing I did not feel was alone during those recovery days. While I remained in the hospital for the next two weeks, my mom came every single day to visit. She didn't know it at the time, but this was the beginning of a ritual she would repeat, on and off, for almost the next three years.

Each morning, she woke up and took care of getting Dad, Pete, Karen, and JoAnne fed and off to work and school. Then she drove to downtown Chicago to be with me in the hospital. She stayed with me until early afternoon, when she would head home to help everyone else after school was over.

Some evenings Dad came to the hospital, when he wasn't traveling for work, and he stayed until visiting hours were over. My parents made sure I never felt cut off from my family during my hospital stays.

COMING HOME

I'll never forget the day I came home from the hospital after my first operation. I had been gone for about two and a half weeks, and I was still recovering from the surgery. I was on some pretty great painkillers when my dad brought me through the front door of the house. As he did, my mom and all of my siblings were right there to welcome me. I was delighted that everyone had set aside their busy schedules to greet me. Then I saw the banner! My brother and sisters had made a sign that stretched almost across the whole living room, and it said "Welcome Home, John!" I was truly amazed. "Wow," I thought. "I think they really missed me!"

Before my first surgery, I would have classified our family life as maybe a little better than average. There were no huge conflicts, mostly because any serious arguments were quickly quelled by my father, who made it very clear that he did not want such openly negative interactions around the house. As a result, Pete and I pretty much lived our lives as the twins, while Karen and JoAnne lived their lives, avoiding too much interference and conflict with each other. This seemed to change for the better after this first of many trips to the hospital. All four of us now seemed to interact more and have a good time together. For the next three months, I continued to recover, and everyone in my family pitched in to help. This continued for the next ten years, until I moved out. I always felt that everyone reached out to me if there was anything I needed. Today I am so thankful for their love and care.

After I came home from that first hospital stay, with severe sight loss and lots of discomfort from the surgery, I really didn't spend lots of time trying to figure out why this had happened to me. In fact, it seemed that this question was on the minds of others much more than it was on mine. I do recall thinking that this whole surgery and eyesight-loss issue was serious and would probably have profound ramifications for maybe several years to come, but I still believed it would all clear up eventually. After all, I had shown myself to be a pretty good kid—I had the teachers' notes and report cards to prove it. Based on my understanding of God and the world around me, this couldn't be some kind of retribution for poor or unsatisfactory behavior. It was pretty easy to look around and see others who were not following the rules as well as I was! And if that was not enough, the newspaper and evening news had tons of others that were off the charts with bad behavior.

My biggest concern that first time I came home was my physical appearance. Not only was all my hair gone, there were bandages up and down my neck. Plus I was on some kind of medication that caused me to retain water and made me bloated. I was very disturbed that I now looked fat. I remember being very self-conscious when a small group of girls from school stopped by my house to say hi. But it also made me feel really good that they thought enough of me to visit!

GETTING BY

I never went back to school that second semester of seventh grade. For three months following the operation, my mom drove me back to the hospital each day for a radiation zap of the operation area. This was a precautionary move the doctors wanted, based on the small chance of an undiscovered tumor in the problem area. When those treatments were completed, we launched into trying to get me caught up with my classes at school. My mom read me the books and assignments, some tutors came to the house each day, and we worked out modified final exams for each of my classes so I could hopefully resume school in the fall in the eighth grade with Pete and my other classmates.

Those weeks at home were the first time

I remember asking my folks questions like, "What am I going to do when it's time for high school?" and "What am I going to do when it's time to take driver's ed?" I had lots of other questions like this too. I remember my dad simply answering, "We're not going to worry about those things right now. We just need to figure out what to do for that next class next semester." So, if he wasn't that worried about all these unknowns in the future, I decided I wasn't going to worry about them either.

My dad had always been in control of the family, and everything had worked out. So I pretty much just stood by while my parents did lots of checking with teachers, administrators, and who knows who else, to figure out what had to be done next. Today, I know there was a great deal of uncertainty, fear, and doubt about my future, but they never indicated that to me, and that's exactly what I needed!

When summer arrived, I lamented that my sailing days were over because of my sight loss. But my dad said, "Why can't you sail? You're not at a greater disadvantage than anyone else. No one else can see the wind either." I don't think he was trying to be particularly profound or philosophical, but those words were exactly the wisdom I needed to hear. It would have been so easy to just write off sailing because of my eyesight, and no one would have argued. Instead, I embraced it and became the sailing expert in my family. I even joined the sailing club in college and crewed during some real regatta races. It wasn't that I was a great sailor—it was that I was scrawny and light, and I didn't cry when the captain yelled at me!

Today I continue to sail on Lake Michigan when we vacation there in the summer. It's one of my most favorite things to do. I've even found technology to fill my need for a live crew member, which is necessary because I can't see my way back to the beach near our cottage. I now have a talking GPS that speaks to me every 15 seconds and tells me how far I am from the shore and what direction our beach is from my boat.

᭣᭢᭣᭢

Also over the summer between seventh and eighth grade, Pete, my dad, and I went to the bicycle store and bought a new tandem. For the next five years, Pete would be the driver of our tandem riding back and forth to school. What should be noted is that Pete gave up the use of a brand new five-speed bicycle he'd gotten just the summer before for his birthday. He had a cool sports car of bikes, but he was suddenly thrust into the role of bus driver for his twin brother. He never grumbled or complained once to me about this new responsibility. The tandem was the only bike of its type at the River Forest Junior High, and it made us sort of celebrities. But even then I knew what a huge favor this was for Pete to do.

That summer was also the first time my shunt failed. One morning, my family had great difficulty waking me up. When I finally responded, I acted like I was in some kind of drugged-out state. They popped me in the car and rushed up to Illinois Masonic Medical Center where Dr. Pawl removed the first shunt and put in another one. After a couple days, I came home and the recuperation began again.

WHAT I HAD NEVER SEEN BEFORE

It began to dawn on me what an enormous blessing my parents and siblings were, and especially my twin brother. It's fair to say I had never before fully appreciated the fact that each and every day of my life was spent in the companionship of a best friend. We did Cub Scouts together. We did six years of Little League together. We went to church and Sunday School together, and we served as altar boys together. In sixth grade, when we were the defensive ends of the football team, the coach had nicknamed us his "Nordic bookends."

I had never been at a strange place with no one to play with—Pete was always there. There was never a time when I felt picked on or singled out for chores around the house—

because Pete always had to do them with me. There was never a night when I had to go to bed by myself in a dark, scary room—Pete was always there having to do the same. And now I had a companion with me to face all the new challenges and changes that were to come.

If anyone had asked me the question "Gosh, why do you think this happened to you?" during my teenage years, I'm sure I would have answered "I don't know!" and shrugged my shoulders. To me, it was a mystery. I just figured it would take time for my eyesight to return. After all, it didn't go away all at one time so it seemed to make sense that it would take time to return. I know I held on to this belief for many years, and I know it got me through a lot of tough times, but it wasn't true. My eyesight would never get better again.

And, unfortunately, the shunt would fail many more times over the next couple of years. The details are a little fuzzy to me, but I do know my memories of these times and my parents' memories are quite different. As we've tried to recount these experiences over the years since, I've realized that my parents remember from the perspective of people who are expected to protect their child from harm and pain. And in instances when that's not possible, they're supposed to do whatever they can to solve the problem. But in my case, my parents could do neither.

A couple times, we were vacationing in Michigan when a seizure occurred, and my dad had some interesting encounters with the state police as he sped back to the hospital two hours away. One time we were pulled over by a state trooper, but when my dad told him we were on the way to the emergency room, and the trooper saw my mom holding me in the backseat, he turned on his lights and siren and led my dad the rest of the way to the hospital—at well over 90 miles an hour!

Each time I would be rushed into the operating room to have one shunt removed from my neck and a replacement shunt put in. Each time it was unclear whether I would survive the operation. The doctors told my parents they did not know why the shunts were failing. Although it was risky, taking out the old one and replacing it was the only option they had. Then I would wake up, and everyone would wait to see how much additional eyesight I had lost.

This was obviously extremely stressful for my parents, but from my point of view, I would go to bed just fine, like any normal night. Then when I woke up, I would be in the intensive care unit of the hospital again. (It was like a bad version of Bill Murray in *Groundhog Day*!) Although the surroundings were vaguely familiar, there would be lots of unexplained pain and discomfort again, and lots of strangers milling around. And maybe most unsettling, all the hair on my head would be gone again!

But either my mom or my dad would always be in my hospital room when I came out of intensive care. Their presence right after the operations was a huge comfort to me. And because they were there with me so much, all that time in the hospital became our experience, not just mine. There must have been a lot of times when I couldn't take medication for some reason, because one of my most vivid memories is of my mom and my dad putting cold washcloths on my forehead to ease the pain.

LEARNING A NEW LANGUAGE

When I returned to junior high at the start of eighth grade, Pete and I had all the same classes. Unfortunately, I was not in class very much because my shunt failed three times during my eighth grade year. I tried a couple of times to return, but most of my schoolwork that year was done at home with the help of my mom and tutors. When I was at school, I was still getting used to my very blurry vision, so my movements around the building were slow and tentative. But at least I was familiar with the hallways because I had been there the year before.

I remember one time sitting with a classmate who asked me how I was reading my books. I told him my books were read to me by my mom or played on on reel-to-reel tape so I could listen to them. "Oh, you're lucky!" he exclaimed. "I wish I could just listen to my books." I didn't say anything, but I wanted to tell him it wasn't as great as it sounded. However, I think he was trying to be nice and positive about the situation.

Also during eighth grade, my teachers realized I needed to learn Braille in order to continue successfully with my education. To do so, it was arranged that I would go twice a week by cab from the River Forest Junior High to a grade school in Berwyn. This is where Mrs. Palmer taught me how to read and write Braille.

The process was slow at first. Each Braille cell consists of six raised dots. Which of the six dots are raised in any particular cell tells you what letter or symbol (like a contraction or punctuation mark) that cell represents. At first, my finger would have to circle the cell over and over until I could perceive which dots were raised. Then, slowly, my fingers got more sensitive and the Braille cells became more clear. By the time I left Mrs. Palmer, I could read a page of the Braille, but not much faster than a second grader reads print. Nevertheless, I thought of this as a huge accomplishment. I used Braille for the rest of my academic career and even depend on it now in my job. (I've gotten a little faster at reading Braille since then!)

Despite this major leap, the most meaningful thing that happened to me at that school in Berwyn was meeting John and Carolyn Novotny. John was just a year younger than I was, and Carolyn was a couple years younger than him. The Novotnys were smart, they were fun, and they were just as friendly as I was. The difference was they had both been born without eyes.

Long before grade school, they had been fitted with glass eyes and never seemed uncomfortable about their appearance or lack of eyesight. I thought about all that I'd enjoyed in my early years: playing sports and games, and finding school pretty easy. Meeting John and Carolyn, I realized they'd never had any of those experiences, and it made me ashamed that I'd thought of my blurred vision as some kind of big deal. As the adage goes, "I felt sorry for myself because I had no shoes until I met a man who had no feet."

Soon after that I started to recognize how blessed I was to still have some sight. More importantly, I realized that if I'd been born a decade or two earlier, I would probably be dead because the technology that saved my life would not have been invented yet!

❧❧❧❧

About a year after my first operation, our family expanded when my third sister, Mary Christine, was born in December 1969. I did not remember much about Karen and JoAnne being born and growing up, so I found MC's birth a fun and unique experience. Also, her arrival seemed to finally take everyone's focus off of me! I was glad for this because I was tired of the spotlight it seemed people thought they had to keep on me. At one point I actually believed MC's birth was a deliberate move by God to emphasize that life would go on. There was a new and exciting life in our midst now—not just mine that seemed full of limits.

HIGH SCHOOL

INTRODUCTION TO OPRF

When Pete and I moved on to Oak Park-River Forest (OPRF) High School, my problems with failing shunts continued. After every return from the hospital to put in a new shunt, which I'd done five times now, everyone hoped the newest replacement would work. The surgery and technology being used was all pretty new, so there wasn't much history of past operations to reference. I made three trips to Illinois Masonic during my freshman year to change shunts. Because there were no tests to tell the doctors anything, I just came in and had surgery to remove the old shunt and implant a new one. Then I rested in the hospital for a couple days, and then went home for several additional days of rest.

My freshman year ended up being two

semesters of three weeks off and six weeks on. Dr. Pawl says now it was amazing that I didn't develop an infection from all the operations during eighth and ninth grade. Still, every operation could have been the one that finally worked, so once I started to recover, everyone focused on getting me back into the mainstream. This meant signing up for classes and working to get all my textbooks for the next semester taped.

Getting through eighth grade had shown me I was qualified and capable enough to get through classes, even with these surgeries and my failing eyesight. Pete continued to be there for me, and the faculty proved themselves willing to cooperate with the accommodations I needed.

MY DEAN FOR LIFE

Another important person who now entered my life during high school was Al Ogden, Pete's and my dean for our four years at OPRF. Mr. Ogden and I would have met regardless of my vision problem, as deans were assigned to students based on the spelling of their last name. However, Mr. Ogden and I had a unique relationship, unlike any other student and dean at the school, as my issues made me unlike any student the school had ever had.

As junior high was wrapping up for me, my parents must certainly have visited OPRF to scope out the dean I would be assigned to and discuss how feasible it was for me to attend the local high school and succeed there. In 1970, Illinois State Law dictated that high school students with visual disabilities be transported from their home each day to the "regional high school equipped for students with visual impairments." This would have meant a 40-minute cab ride back and forth to a high school 24 miles away from home every day. What made these schools "equipped" was that they had a resource teacher on staff who was qualified to work with students with visual impairments.

The fact that Pete would be attending school as well, although maybe not having every class with me, had to be a big factor in everyone deciding to let me give OPRF a try. Both my parents were graduates of OPRF, and they wanted me to remain a part of the community, not go away to another high school. They knew how nice it was to attend a neighborhood school, as it was less than a mile away from our house and even walkable during the spring and fall. And, in the back of their minds, they knew that being closer to home would be critical if the shunt were to fail during school. Luckily, all the remaining seizures and trips to Illinois Masonic occurred at night.

Knowing Mr. Ogden as I do today, I'm sure my situation represented a bit of a personal challenge to him. He was the kind of dean who did everything in his power for the best interest of the student, even if that meant going outside accepted standards or practices. He was very popular with both his students and their parents. I heard this from other classmates quite a bit. So, between my parents and Mr. Ogden, I had a mighty alliance of support to give OPRF a try.

I visited Mr. Ogden's office many, many times during my years at OPRF, but I distinctly remember one of my first trips there. The deans' offices were set up in clumps at the high school. When a student entered the office, he checked in with a receptionist and then took a seat until his dean was able to see him. While I was waiting, I couldn't help but overhear Mr. Ogden speaking to a student in his office, and he was not a happy camper! The girl had obviously been to his office with problems before, and she was there now because she had refused to behave the way Dean Ogden had told her she must. His words were forceful and no nonsense, but he did not cross over the line to a yell. Nonetheless, he seemed to be in such a foul mood that I considered getting up and coming back some other time. But I stayed. When it was my turn to go in, I sheepishly entered with some kind of salutation like, "I'm really sorry to bother you, Mr. Ogden, but..."

But his greeting to me was positive and upbeat! There was no sign that his difficult prior meeting was going to influence mine. Nevertheless, that early glimpse of him left an impression that caused me to always begin our meetings with an apology for taking up his time. This persisted until one day when I arrived and he abruptly stopped me from talking. In the closest voice to a shout that I ever heard from him, he said, "For Pete's sake, stop apologizing every time you come in here!" Although I was tempted to say "I'm sorry for apologizing all the time," I don't think I did.

His statement had a profound impact on my self-perception. It made me realize my visual problem was not my fault, and that people might not always feel inconvenienced when dealing with me. In many cases, such as Mr. Ogden's, dealing with my vision problem was as much a part of their responsibilities as it was mine. This was a huge step! Although being legally blind was a bit more unique and off the beaten path of physical maladies, it wasn't any more special or difficult to deal with than a person with a mobility problem, or even learning disability. It was just different.

During my four years in high school, Mr. Ogden was my wise and benign counsel and benefactor. I am sure that he, behind the scenes, met with my teachers before the semester began and made sure they were willing and able to adapt their teaching to accommodate me—and this was no easy task. First of all, there was my Brailler: a ten-pound contraption I carried from class to class and took my notes with. As I did so, it made a *kachung, kachung* noise with each character I typed, and it ended each line with a bing! Then I would manually push the line-up button and return the point of the Braille writer to the beginning of the line. Being in a class with me meant enduring a constant chorus of *kachung, kachung, kachung, kachung, bing, zip, click!* I am deeply grateful to all my teachers and fellow students who put up with that. It comforts me to think that today's visually impaired students probably use talking laptops with ear plugs or some other technology that's less disruptive to those around them.

From the first day I attended classes at OPRF, finding my classrooms and making my way through the crowded hallways of the school were huge challenges. Luckily, Mr. Ogden helped me get my schedule of classes prior to the first day of school, and he got me access to the school so I could map out the best way to move from class to class in advance. Without this, trying to move through the hallways to my classrooms with 4000 other students would have been impossible in the few minutes allowed.

THE TEACHER
WHO KNEW THE ROPES

Patricia Burrows was the resource teacher at Proviso West High School in the early 1970s. She is another important person in my life I would never have met if not for my visual impairment. Proviso was the high school I was supposed to attend as a visually impaired student, and I suspect that Mrs. Burrows is the person who eventually signed off on the decision to let me attend OPRF. She volunteered to come to OPRF for a couple hours twice a week to help me with anything I needed, rather then me traveling to her school five days a week.

Despite this, my memory is that my time with Mrs. Burrows did not start particularly well. She worked with me a great deal on improving my Braille-reading ability, and I tried to practice between our sessions, but it always seemed that other scholastic responsibilities took up my time.

At the end of my first semester of freshman year, my family took a long driving trip down to Florida. (Luckily, I had just replaced my shunt a couple weeks before we left, so we had good reason to believe that there would not be a shunt failure while we were out of town.) Before I left, I got a Braille book from Mrs. Burrows. It was titled *Animal Farm*. My dad did a lot of the driving at night, and I sat in the front passenger's seat and read my book. My dad looked over at me several times and tried to wake me up because he thought I had fallen asleep, or worse, was having a seizure. My chin was on my chest, but he could not see my hands moving as I read the book on my lap. It's a good thing Mrs. Burrows gave me a book like *Animal Farm* that had an underlying political message, as it kept me wanting to read more of the story and inadvertently kept me practicing my Braille!

When I returned, Mrs. Burrows was amazed at how much my Braille reading had improved. For the next four years, she regularly stopped by my high school and assisted me in many ways. As she did so, I remember thinking that maybe my vision problem would not hold me back in life as much as I'd first thought. I know I was afraid that if I admitted to myself that I was now legally blind, I was accepting a designation that would pretty much institutionalize my life. I would be forced to accept that there were many, many things I would never be able to do, and I didn't want to do that.

When classes began my freshman year, it had only been 18 months since the loss of my sight, and my movements were still tentative. Fortunately, Pete and I had most of our classes together freshman year, so we moved together from class to class. But we had fewer classes in common each year after that. I always had my white cane out when moving from class to class so other students would give me a wider berth when moving past, or at least not punch me if I were to bump into them. However, I was involved in an altercation my freshman year. I was in a hallway, walking to my next class without Pete when a fellow smacked into me from my left side. Before I could muster a humble apology, a second guy grabbed the first guy and threw him against the lockers.

"Hey! Watch where you're going," he yelled.

I immediately recognized the voice of the second guy as Carl from my grade school. Carl was known to all as someone you didn't mess with, but I had always made it a point to be friendly and cordial to him. I never thought he felt any kind of friendship toward me, but now, here he was acting as my hallway bodyguard. Carl turned and motioned for me to continue to my class.

"Hey, thanks!" I said, and proceeded on my way.

Moving around OPRF highlighted one of the paradoxes of being legally blind: I had enough blurred vision to move through the halls without always running into any large, stationary objects or people moving the same direction as I was, but I could not identify anyone's faces. The only way I ever knew that one of the hundreds of people moving around me was someone I knew was if that person said hello to me. And often, just saying the word hello wasn't enough for me to recognize exactly who was talking. In addition, moving through the halls between classes was like being on the Dan Ryan Expressway. There was no way I could stop and casually find out more information. There wasn't even enough time to say "Who's that?" But I never felt comfortable saying that anyway. This basic fact has not changed to this day, but my mobility skills have improved dramatically, so people may very well think I see much better than I do and wonder why I'm never the one to say hi to them.

THE THREE AMIGOS

During high school, There were three friends with whom Pete and I did most things: Kevin, Dave, and Dick. Kevin Hanley had attended Washington grade school with Pete and me, starting in first grade. Kevin had a great sense of humor that sometimes bordered on outrageous. He had an older brother and sister, and I always thought of him as more worldly than I was because of his older siblings. Dave Beeman had also been a friend of ours since very early grade school, but our connection had come through Little League and church. Dave was the oldest child in his family, just like me, but he always seemed to know more about what was going on around us. Pete and I met Dick Mason when we moved to Roosevelt grade school in sixth grade. We never played

Little League on any of Dick's teams, but he was good friends with several other guys in the class that we did know from Little League, and we just hit it off right away. Dick had a very down-home type of humor, and he was the third in a family of four boys. Dick was also the oldest of any of us so he got his driver's permit first, and there was always an available car at his place.

It was also fun to go to Dick's house because it was Testosterone City there: a place teeming with all the stuff guys like. This included food to eat, Coke to drink, and the hottest music. This latter item was of particular interest to Pete, who had a love and appreciation for cutting edge music of the time. The music I liked was either 5 or 10 years old or bubblegum pop music. While Pete's album collection included Santana, The Who, and Led Zeppelin, among the few albums I had were The Cowsills and The Monkees. However, I did maintain a speck of respect by appreciating many of the early Beatles hits.

Kevin, Dave, and Dick all learned how to watch a movie from the fifth row of the theater while we were in high school together. Sitting that close enabled me to catch the major movements and theme of most movies, although there always were a handful of questions I had to ask like, "What did that subtitle just say?" or "Who was that guy who just spoke?" They were all great sports to make that accommodation for me.

But far and away the best example of someone going the extra mile for me was when Pete went with me to see *Das Boot*. The movie was the story of a German U-boat crew during the Second World War, and it was all in German, with English subtitles. Pete knew I wanted to see it badly, so we went, found some seats away from others, and he proceeded to read the whole movie for me! Ironically, the movie ended up being so successful in the United States that a dubbed English version came out a year or so later.

As far as keeping ourselves entertained, simply driving to someone else's house to see what they were doing was the regular routine. Interspersed throughout were sorties to downtown Chicago, about 10 miles away, where we would pick up pizza or, on a big night, attend a show at The Second City. And if we didn't want to drive far for food, there was always Peterson's Ice Cream Parlor in Oak Park, which was just three blocks from both my house and Dick's house. Because I could never help with the driving, I was always looking for ways to contribute to the evening out. When my friends discovered this, we always made sure my white cane was prominently displayed when we asked for a restaurant table or seats at the theater. I was proud that my cane got us the best seats in the house on a regular basis!

MY BEST NEW FRIEND IN HIGH SCHOOL WAS BLOND

Though I was thankful for these long-standing friendships, I did, of course, make some new friends in high school as well. The first of several people who would become great friends of mine, and who I never would have met if not for my visual impairment, was Cindy Dillon. I met Cindy when I started my freshman year. Dean Ogden had realized that the conventional study halls students had during the school day would be of no help to me. Not only would I need lots of space for my Braille writer, magic markers, reams of scratch paper, and reel-to-reel tape player to listen my taped textbooks, I would need privacy to listen to them, and I would often need an actual person to read to me handouts and other materials I could not get taped. So Mr. Ogden coordinated most of my study halls each week to match up with Cindy's, and he commandeered a small storage closet for me to go to with Cindy during my study halls. I never did ask her if she was asked to volunteer for my reading job, or if she was able to use it as something on her college applications, perhaps as an extracurricular, public service activity. Quite frankly, I never cared why she was there—I was just glad she was.

When we first met, Cindy was a junior and on her way to becoming one of her class's valedictorians. Of much more interest to me, I thought she was gorgeous! Not only was Cindy smart, she was nice, friendly, easy to talk to—and she was blond. She was an enormous help to me scholastically during my first two years of high school, especially freshman year when I was trying to get my feet on the ground in this new environment. She also had another significant influence on me: Although we never dated, she was the reason I found myself dating only blond women for the next ten years, and finally marrying one!

Cindy never called me John. Her name for

me was Juanito. I was flattered by her use of such a friendly and familiar nickname, and it stuck for as long as we knew each other. My room, as I came to call it, was on the third floor of the high school, just off one of the major staircases. Its ten-by-eight-foot dimensions were just large enough to handle a table a little bigger than a card table and two chairs. In one corner, a six-inch pipe ran from the floor to the ceiling. Although I was initially assigned a locker like all other freshman, I never used it once I realized my room would do a better job of serving as my locker too. Within the first week of school, a self-standing coat hanger and very small end table found their way to my room.

But the nicest touch came during my second semester when Cindy bought me a poster: a view of a man entering a manhole, from inside the manhole. We borrowed scotch tape from one of the teachers and proceeded to affix the poster to the ceiling of my room. After that we could pretend we were working in the sewer. In later years I added one or two other posters to the walls of my room, but I never took down Cindy's poster, which I cherished.

I never decorated or put any kind of marking on the outside door of my room, as I relished its privacy and clandestine nature. There were more than a couple times that good friends asked me if they could borrow the key to my room to take a nap after some kind of long night before.

My sessions with Cindy were primarily business: reading handouts from teachers and reviewing my lessons and homework. But we always found a couple free minutes to talk about dances and things that were going on. Cindy shared just enough information about her social life for me to know she didn't sit around the house much at night and never missed a Prom or homecoming dance.

LAST RITES AT 16

Very early in my sophomore year, I had another seizure and returned to Illinois Masonic Medical Center. Many years later, my father told me it was then that Dr. Pawl told him and my mother the very grim news that there was no sense in replacing the shunt anymore. It wasn't working, and the doctors didn't know why. There was nothing else they could do to make me better, and it would not be long before I passed away. So, Father O'Connor, a priest from St. Luke's, our church, and a close friend of my parents, came to the hospital and gave me the Sacrament of Last Rites.

I was now unconscious due to the seizure from the pressure on the brain. Because I wouldn't suffer no matter what happened, now, Dr. Pawl asked my parents' permission to do one more exploratory operation. He wanted to try an experimental shunt procedure in the back of my neck. It had been tried on a few others, but discontinued as too risky for the potential benefit in every way. However, with no options remaining, my parents agreed.

"When [Dr. Pawl] opened you up, the pressure just poured out, and your vital signs started to come back," my dad recently told me. So during this operation, not only was the shunt that ran down the right side of my neck replaced, but a second shunt was inserted that ran down the back of my head. This second shunt would be dangerously close to my spinal cord, and the risks of something going wrong were great, but there were no better ideas. (Dr. Pawl told me this many years later.)

"After that procedure you came back pretty strong, and even though I think we all thought it would again be just temporary, we were glad to have whatever time with you the Good Lord intended you to have," my dad later told me.

"While all this was going on, and all the way through your recovery, you can imagine how many times your mother made the trip back and forth [to the hospital] while still managing to take care of and give as comfortable a home life as possible to your brother and sisters," he added. "[She made sure] their lives did not come to a standstill."

That experimental procedure proved to be a stroke of genius, and that was the ninth and last operation I needed to replace a shunt.

I had tried to keep thinking my eyesight would come back someday if I gave the shunts enough time to work. Surely all these accommodations like Braille and books on tape were just a short-term fix. But now it had been three years since that first operation, and my eyesight was not better. It was a lot worse. My right eye was totally blind now, and the vision in my left eye was like being surrounded in heavy fog. In the very center of that eye, the fog was so thick I could not see anything through it. The bottom left quadrant of that eye was where the fog was the thinnest. Although I was still unable to read any kind of printed type, I could see things like a thick magic marker writing in 2-inch-high letters, or the contrast of a dark mountain against the sky many miles away.

My eyesight remains like this today. But it

hasn't gotten worse, and the trips to the hospital and operations are over!

REBUILDING TIME FOR BIG JOHN

Sophomore year at OPRF now became the beginning of my "rebuilding era." My grades started to improve steadily, and all the efforts to catch up and stay on track with school began to build on each other, as they would continue to do. Mr. Ogden even put Pete and me into a handful of Honors and Advanced Placement classes. These succeeded in restoring my confidence in my academic abilities.

Along with my self-perception, another of my first rebuilding experiences at OPRF was to improve my physical condition. Since freshman year, I had been assigned to the pool for physical education, primarily to satisfy the state's requirement for swimming. For the rest of high school, I regularly attended the remedial training class, where mostly injured athletes worked with progressive resistance machines. I really enjoyed this opportunity to add some weight by adding muscle—as I knew so well, thanks to my junior high gym teacher.

By my sophomore year, my relationship with Mr. Ogden had matured quite a bit. He was a facilitator for me—lending advice and influence to my challenges at the high school. I don't think I'd been a helpless, clueless freshman either, as he regularly addressed me as "Big John, Big John, Big Bad John." This was, of course, right from the Jimmy Dean song of that time, but that wasn't the kind of music my friends and I were listening to, so the full cleverness of the greeting was not completely appreciated until many years later when all songs of that time period became favorites of mine!

Also during sophomore year, Dad and I experienced the only unsuccessful accommodation attempt for me that I can ever remember. It was clear to everyone that the onset of driver's ed for Pete and all my friends had made me slightly depressed. Dad had an idea that I could back out our family car from the garage to the front of the house. So, he and I had some dry-run lessons in the car regarding the gearshift, brake, and gas pedal. I learned to start the car, put it in gear, and by cracking the driver's side door, I could see and follow the edge of the driveway out to the front of the house. The whole time, someone would watch to make sure no person or pets got in harm's way.

After a couple successful runs, our friend Kevin came to the house one night to go to the movies. While Pete made sure no one was in the way, I started to back the car out. I was beside the house when Kevin came running. He shouted that I should stop, put the car in park, and get out so he could drive. I put the car in what I thought was park and started to climb out. But the car was in reverse, and as I tried to exit, it started rolling backward! Kevin couldn't reach the brake because I was in the way, so the car gently swerved and rolled into our house with the worst scraping noise! That ended my driving for a long time.

By this time, I had been using my closed circuit television camera (CCTV) at home for three years. The CCTV had become my primary electronic tool to aid with reading. It sat on a tabletop and had a movable tray about 15 inches square. Mounted above the tray was a television camera that pointed straight down and took a picture of an area about one inch big, then blew it up onto a 15-inch television monitor that sat next to the tray. This enlarged printed type enough for me to read it, so it was great for reading typed letters, soup can instructions, and prescription bottles.

For three years, I had not built any model tanks or planes because of my sight. I could no longer see the parts. But I decided I would buy a simple model and try to use the CCTV to build it. To my delight, it worked just fine. It was, of course, a very long and tedious process since I had to read the instructions, identify which parts of the model to needed, find them on the racks of model parts, then glue them together—all with the help of the CCTV. I repeated these steps over and over and over again until the model was complete. But the inconvenience didn't matter. I was so excited to discover a way to recapture a part of my life I'd thought was lost forever. Today, building models is my favorite at-home pastime.

❧❧❧❧

It was also during my sophomore year at OPRF that a unique opportunity came up. The student who'd been elected our sophomore class president moved away early in the year. There was going to be a special election to elect a new president. I happened to ask Mr. Ogden what kind of responsibilities there were for such an elected position, and he told me there were very few responsibilities for the president of the class during the sophomore year. He detected that I had some interest, and he assured me that I had all the ability needed to do such a job, so I ran for the office.

It was a lucky thing for me that River Forest Junior High was the largest school that fed into OPRF. Most students were still just beginning to make friends with students from the Oak Park junior highs, so I think more students recognized my name and voted for me because of that. It was just like those elections for judges when you know nothing about the actual people, so you vote for the only familiar name you see! And perhaps my operations during freshman year gave me the sympathy vote too. But like any true politician would say: You do whatever it takes to get the votes. It doesn't matter how!

Mr. Ogden showed me that my life was not going to stop just because I was legally blind. This is what my parents had also tried so hard to show me, but I needed an outside authority to confirm it. Mr. Ogden and Mrs. Burrows always acted as though my future was going to be no different than that of most students at OPRF: I would get through there and go on to complete college too. My four years with them were the time I needed to build my confidence in what I could do, rather than focus on the things I'd had to leave behind. With the help of my parents, Mr. Ogden, Mrs. Burrows, Pete, and my friends, I realized my life could be not that much different than anyone else's. I would just need a little help around the edges.

Still, it was impossible to avoid the fact that participating in sports with Pete and my friends was a thing of the past. I could still follow sports and attend games with friends, but I would no longer be playing them myself. During high school, I always went with Pete and my friends to any of the Cubs games, Sox games, and even Blackhawk games in Chicago they were going to. I learned to take a transistor radio with me so I could listen to the play-by-play while being right at the game.

I'd also learned that working outside the system was sometimes best. Before my eyesight challenges began, I was content to accept all the rules and parameters put upon me. After all, I believed the rules had been made by the experts, and for a reason, even if I didn't know what that reason was. I'd found that working within the rules pleased most people in authority, and this was the best way to get ahead. But now, after my experiences in high school, I was starting to understand that sometimes new ideas and new ways of doing things could be better than the current, sanctioned way. This was a big step for me.

PART TWO OF MY SPIRITUAL JOURNEY

Some time during our sophomore year, Pete and I were invited to a Young Life meeting by a couple of our friends. Young Life is a non-denominational Christian youth group that has weekly meetings at people's houses. The meetings were about an hour long and consisted of about half an hour of singing, 15 or so minutes of skits and funny stuff, and a message about Jesus at the end. This was unlike any religious activity I had ever participated in, and I really liked it. The music was beautiful, as the singing was dominated by the girls there, and the skits were often slapstick in nature—totally different from church.

Our family continued to regularly attend church at St. Luke's during high school, and

Pete's and my participation in Young Life with our friends did not mean that our time at the Catholic church was cut back at all. Going to church as a family was important to everyone in my family, and it was to me too. But Young Life was my first glimpse of how other Christians live their lives, so I was very interested. Here was a place where you could have fun and laugh and still be participating in something spiritual. Prior to this, I'd felt that anytime I found myself having lots of fun, I was probably doing something wrong. The final messages at Young Life always had a Jesus focus to them, and I became interested in learning more about why friends and acquaintances from other Christian denominations did not seem to have as structured or rigorous a formula for living life.

MY RETURN TO SPORTS

One day during my sophomore year in high school, Mrs. Burrows asked me if I was interested in downhill skiing. She told me there was a new organization called the American Blind Skiing Foundation (ABSF), and they were looking for people to join. I had never done downhill skiing before I lost my sight, so I told her I probably wasn't qualified. But she said that didn't matter. She thought they would teach me. So I decided to give it a try.

Apart from Young Life, I was not involved in many other activities at that time. Keeping up with classes seemed to take up a huge part of my day. Because I had to listen to my books on tape, rather than reading them, I used to figure that if a teacher said she was assigning an hour of reading homework, I could count on it taking me one and a half to two hours to complete.

But that night I went home and told my parents about ABSF. A little bit to my surprise, my dad seemed really excited to hear about the program. I realize now that he was very involved with finding answers to the limitations I faced every day. He was always looking for opportunities for me to try new things. He'd made sure I could still sail at the cottage, he'd tried his best to get me behind the wheel of a car, and now he was eagerly supportive of skiing. He never showed me any of the worry or despair he might have been feeling, and I know his positive attitude was contagious to me. Hey, if my dad wasn't worried or depressed about this whole debacle, I wasn't going to be either! I trusted him, and if he thought skiing was worth trying, I was on board.

However, that's not to say I didn't have down days too. There were nights when I was very frustrated that my taped reading took so long to get through. And because I'd just learned to read Braille a couple years before, it took lots of extra time to review my notes. But there was no giving up, because I didn't want to slip a year behind Pete. I wanted us both to leave home for college at the same time.

Anyway, within just a couple of weeks, my dad and I drove about an hour away to a small ski resort called Four Lakes to the west of Chicago. As we got closer, I got more and more excited to give the whole thing a try. I really got enthused when we went to the ski rental area and fitted ourselves with all the equipment. *This is like being a gladiator*, I thought. The program organizers had gathered a group of professional ski instructors to serve as teachers and one-on-one guides for the blind skiers, but because so many blind skiers had showed up—more than anyone seemed to have expected—about half of us had to sit out either the morning or the afternoon while the limited number instructors worked with the rest of skiers. I was one of the lucky skiers to go out first, and I loved it!

Every skier worked with his or her own guide. Both the skier and guide wore bright orange bibs that said either Blind Skier or Guide so other skiers wouldn't assume we could see and avoid them, if necessary. Instead they would give us plenty of space. Then, depending on how much sight the skier actually had, the guide would either lead her down the hill or ski behind him and give vocal commands all the way down.

When you're teaching someone with a visual impairment, you can't just say, "Watch me and do it this way." As I like to put it, you have to teach from the inside out. For skiing, this means not saying "bend your knee like this," but "bend your knee so you feel your shin against the tongue of your boot," or "keep your arms bent while skiing, as if you're carrying a tray down the slope." This definitely makes the teaching a bit more challenging.

I much preferred that the guide ski in front of me and I follow down the hill. Even though all the skiing that first day took place on either flat ground or the bunny hill, the feeling of moving while making small adjustments to change speed and direction felt like finally being part of driver's education. Now, with ABSF, I was doing driving of my own!

Another great thing about ABSF is that it gave me an opportunity to connect with John and Carolyn Novotny again, my old friends from Braille classes in Berwyn. Learning to ski for me was like skiing during a whiteout storm. I couldn't see the bumps in the snow or even tell which way was downhill or uphill, but I could distinguish the dark shapes of people and trees against the white snow. Yet I knew John and Carolyn could not. Despite that, they were two of the best skiers that participated with ABSF in those early years. As a matter of fact, both John and Carolyn went on to ski in races across the country. John eventually moved to Colorado and got married there.

Several years ago, I was very sad to hear that John had a brain tumor. He died not too long after that. I continue to thank God that He introduced me to John and Carolyn so soon after I experienced my sight loss. They were great friends and helped me put my life, and my "visual inconvenience" in perspective at a relatively young age.

Anyway, ABSF offered ski opportunities almost every weekend, January through mid March, and they released a schedule of their planned dates and locations. But they never got any more instructors, so there was always the half-day of waiting for some of the skiers.

After Dad and I participated in the program

for several weeks, some of the ABSF leaders took note of how well we moved together to and from the ski area and within the ski lodge. Since the first days of my sight loss, we had become accustomed to walking together, and we now moved very quickly. The ABSF leaders asked my dad if he would consider trying to be a ski guide for me.

Now, my dad had not skied a day in his life. However, we also were not talking about skiing at high speeds in those early days. So, he slapped on a pair of skis and a bright orange guide bib, and we took off. At this time, my dad was about 46 years old. Only when I reached the age of 46 myself did the true scope of my dad's courage, love, and dedication to me really sink in! The leaders of ABSF took note of our progress too. During my second or third season of skiing, the small number of professional ski instructors was gradually replaced by a full compliment of solid, intermediate-skiing volunteers. I don't think any skier in the program would dispute that the key to a safe, fun, successful day of skiing is more dependent on the trust and communication between skier and guide than the skiing proficiency of the guide.

Skiing had an enormous effect on my self-confidence. It also signaled my re-entry into sports. Later in high school, and again in both college and graduate school, I joined friends and went skiing with them, using all the techniques and procedures ABSF had taught me. Many times a friend would remark, "Wow, you can ski?" And each time I answered, "Yeah!" I believed it more and more. I suddenly realized I'd written off skiing as something I could never do because of my sight. Now, since I could ski, I began to realize there were probably lots of other things I could do too.

❧❧❧❧

A final note about my sophomore year of high school, which was quite a momentous one for me: Cindy, my faithful reader and friend, graduated at the end of my sophomore year, and she went on to Wesleyan College and then to graduate school. She and I kept in touch and sometimes got together for lunch when she was back home in Oak Park.

GETTING INTO THE DATING GAME

When my junior year of high school came around, I was finally starting to feel pretty good about myself again. My participation in the gym program since freshman year, as well as skiing, had restored my confidence in my physical abilities. My grades during freshman and sophomore year had been very satisfactory too. The one part of life I felt I was still missing out on was dating.

Some of my friends had girlfriends. In most cases they'd spotted them from afar, called the on the phone, and finally went out on a date with them with using their family's car. I couldn't figure out the logistics of even just finding someone I'd like to go out with. I couldn't see that far. And how would I make the whole date work if I couldn't drive?

I briefly considered asking Pete or one of my friends to help me set up a double date, but that made me feel like some pitiful loser. I wanted to do this myself, and junior Prom gave me the opportunity! All during junior year, I had an American history class where a really cute girl sat behind me. Her name was Karen, and she was sweet, smart, and seemed to enjoy my jokes. Also, needless to say, Karen was a blond. Junior Prom seemed like an event many people would be going to, even if they weren't in a serious relationship. So I got Karen's number and thought out a whole script of not only how I would ask her to the Prom, but also what I would say if she turned me down. Not having something to say at that point would be incredibly awkward, so I wanted that potential covered.

Well, I made the phone call, but an awkward moment appeared anyway. I had nothing to say after she said yes to my invitation. All I could come up with at the spur of the moment was, "Uh, well, I guess I'll be calling you back later, right? Thanks a lot."

Karen and I double dated to the Prom with

my good friend Dick Mason and his girlfriend. The best part of the night was when I boldly asked if Karen wanted to go out again sometime, and she said yes to that question too.

Karen showed me that not being able to drive was no reason not to ask someone out. What I found so enjoyable about dating Karen was being a part of her life, and having her be a part of mine. She lived about nine blocks away, and I simply walked over to her house most of the time.

This sounds easy, of course, but it had been quite a journey to get there. Two years before, my dad had arranged for me to meet with a mobility instructor from the Hines Veterans Hospital to learn about walking with a white cane. I'd been against the idea because I didn't like the idea of calling attention to my visual impairment, but I did it anyway. And now this training was paying off in spades. I could make my own plans and go to Karen's anytime I wanted. I didn't have to wait around helplessly until someone could give me a ride. I was actually less impaired when I used the cane.

Karen and I got together regularly on

Tuesday nights to watch *MASH* on TV. And we attended all the student events and dances at OPRF. However, I think the current generation has a much better general policy about attending most school functions: If you want to go, you just go. You don't have to have a significant other to make you qualified to attend.

Also during my junior year of high school, I got an unexpected upgrade to my at-school study quarters. I came in one Monday morning and found a note on the door of my room telling me to come to Mr. Ogden's office. I went there immediately, and he told me my room had been moved to the fourth floor. When I saw the new room I was amazed. It was four times the size of my old room and even had a skylight! It seems the Oak Park Fire Department had done their standard inspection of the high school over the weekend, and when they came to my room they'd asked why a broom closet was furnished. When they were told a blind student studied there, they didn't like it at all. So, thanks to them, I enjoyed palatial accommodations for the rest of my high school career.

Mr. Ogden also arranged for several other

volunteer readers to assist me during my junior and senior years, but I became much more productive on my own as my high school career progressed. I needed less one-on-one reading help after Cindy's graduation.

☙❧☙❧

During the summer between junior and senior year, I found myself in the mountains of Colorado at a Young Life camp, listening to one of the leaders make his final points on a very emotional sermon regarding Jesus and his death on the cross. "I want each of you to ask yourself: Are you a Christian?" he said. I thought deeply and sincerely answered to myself, "I'm sure trying to be." Then the leader said, "And if you say to yourself, 'I'm trying to be'—then you're not!"

Well, I was stunned and devastated at the same time. How could he say that? I was so upset that I stopped listening to whatever else he had to say. The speaker that night very well may have gone on to do a fine job of explaining what he meant, but I heard none of it. We were soon excused from the talk and encouraged to find a place by ourselves and pray or ponder what we'd heard. I did so and prayed to God that "I did not get at all this idea of 'not trying to be a Christian.' How could any of us ever get to heaven and be with God and Jesus if we never tried? But I also prayed that God would help me figure out what all this was supposed to mean.

I would not find that answer for about six years.

HIGH SCHOOL FINALE

During my senior year of high school, everything finally seemed to come together. It had now been almost two years since my shunt last failed, and I slowly felt a growing sense of confidence in my physical health. Maybe my regular trips to the hospital were finally over! Mr. Ogden helped me pick my final classes to take in high school, and he continued to find other students who were available during my study halls to be readers for me. Pete was now able to use the family car to drive us to high school in the morning, so our tandem bike got a rest.

Karen and I continued dating all year long. We'd rendezvous sometimes in my room during the school day, and we had lunch together most of the time. Her house was the same direction from the high school as mine so we'd also walk home most of the way together.

Going out with Karen was really important for me and my self-perception. Despite my mental and physical improvements, I'd had a nagging doubt that a girl would ever really find me attractive and worth being in a relationship with. I would never be able to drive, or do a lot of other "regular" things because of my eyesight. Karen's friendship was a big help, but that nagging doubt would be with me for many years to come. When college came and we went different ways, the time we'd enjoyed together made it easier for both of us to realize there were a lot of other people in the world we wanted to meet—and who might even want to meet us too.

I saw Karen at our ten-year Oak Park-River Forest High School reunion. She made a point to find me and show me a picture of her baby boy. Though I couldn't see the details of the baby's face, I could tell how happy and proud she was. We quickly caught up on the past ten years, and it was great to see how God had blessed her life too.

One of my last classes at OPRF was creative writing with Mr. McGintey. We learned to write short stories, poems, and limericks. I enjoyed the class and honed my skill at writing different funny words to existing songs, just like my favorite section of Mad magazine. But my best memory of Mr. McGintey's class is that he wrote personal poems to each of us at the end of the semester. For me, Mr. McGintey recorded his note on a cassette tape. He concluded by explaining that the origin of the word goodbye is the phrase "God be with you." And if that were the case, he was very pleased to say "Goodbye, John" at the end of this class.

Almost forty years later, I can tell you his wish came to pass: God has been with me the whole way.

COLLEGE & BEYOND

HERE COME THE IRISH!

When Pete and I began thinking about college, we initially agreed that it was probably a good idea if we went our separate ways and got some experience living with someone else. However, the tools and technology I had in the early 1970s were few compared to what high school kids have today to help them research colleges. I was very ambivalent about where I would go. I knew I wanted a coed campus, because that's what I'd gotten used to at OPRF, and I wanted to make meeting girls as easy as possible! And I did not see any advantage to going to a school that was a lot bigger than OPRF, because it would pose additional challenges in getting around and finding the places I had to be.

Lucky for me, Pete had a very good idea

of where he wanted to go: The University of Notre Dame in South Bend, Indiana. Pete always had been good at athletics, and he had once gone to a Notre Dame football game. He still remembered the spirit and enthusiasm for sports he'd witnessed there. Also, our maternal grandfather, Joe Carroll, had been quite the Notre Dame subway alum (someone who never attended the school, but carries a profound love for it anyway), and Pete had caught much of Grampa Joe's enthusiasm for the school. So, early in our college search process, Pete announced he was going to take a "college day" off from high school and visit Notre Dame. Well, I'd never been to Notre Dame, and I figured visiting any kind of college campus would be helpful to me in making my own college selection, even though I was certain that a big school like Notre Dame would never work for me. Besides, if Pete was going to get a day off of school, I was going to take a day off too! (I think this was part of the competitive "twin mentality" I had grown into over the past 17 years.)

When we visited Notre Dame, I was shocked to discover that there were only 6,000 undergraduate students there. This did not seem like many more than the 4,000 students at OPRF, and at Notre Dame they were all spread out over a large campus, not crammed into a single building. Notre Dame was also just two and a half hours away from home—far enough that I would not be tempted to run home during a crisis, but close enough to make holiday travel pretty easy. So my feelings about attending Notre Dame changed pretty quickly. However, Pete and I did stick with our agreement that we would not live together, even if we went to the same school. Living apart was probably the biggest experiment in this whole college experience.

We were both accepted by Notre Dame, and we were delighted! Pete decided quickly he wanted to have the traditional experience of Notre Dame, so he chose Morrissey Hall as his dorm. It was very close to the "archie building" where architecture students studied and took their classes. Pete knew from the very beginning that he was going to be an architecture major at Notre Dame, or an "archie," as they were called. I, on the other hand, always felt that Morrissey, like many of the other traditional dorms, was a bit Spartan. (During the winter months, the only way to regulate the temperature in any particular room was to adjust how much your one outside window was cracked open.)

During one of my subsequent visits to Notre Dame during the summer after my senior year of high school, I came to campus to choose a dorm. We visited several of the older dorms first. None of these had air conditioning, and none were very comfortable in the middle of summer. However, one of the two newer, high-rise dorms, Flanner, was very different from the others. It was eleven stories high, had elevators for students to use, and most importantly, it was air conditioned! The decision was a lay-up: I was going to live in Flanner.

❧❧❧❧

When the fall came, Pete and I packed up the car and drove with my parents to Notre Dame. We were greeted by students who offered to help us unpack and move in. At Flanner Hall, one of the students who offered his help was Ross Browner, a Notre Dame football player on his way to greatness in both his college and professional football career! I am about 5 feet, 8 inches tall, and I remember several times being on the elevator with Ross and other ND football players. I pretty much looked at their belt buckles or stomachs when I glanced over at them.

My new roommate was a nice guy, and we got along just fine, but he wasn't very adventurous. He knew what his major was going to be (I did not), and he knew what he was going to do in his free time (I did not). I wanted to go wandering around to meet people and check out places, but he did not. I realized I would have to depend on Pete or someone else to help me meet others and fully discover what Notre Dame and college life had to offer.

But, my immediate need was to get my arms around the demands of my classes and professors, and this did not go well at first. Unlike OPRF, there was no Mr. Ogden to help me plan classes, brief professors about me, or set up volunteer readers to handle the overflow of reading materials beyond the books I had already gotten recorded. There was no Department of Student Services at Notre Dame back then.

During my first week of classes, I had chemistry, which had been recommended for me, despite my reservations. The class met in a large auditorium room. I took notes with my Brailler, which made its usual *kachung, kachung, bing, click, zip* noises. After class, the professor came to me and said my machine was disrupting the students around me and I would have to find another way to take notes. So I tried to switch from taking Braille notes to writing them with a magic marker. This wasn't easy, but I did it for a whole semester. And then it dawned on me: this was ridiculous! So I did not take a second semester of chemistry, but switched to biology instead—something I would have thought unconscionable just six months earlier.

That ended up being the most significant A-ha! moment of my college career. I realized no one was going to tell me the answers to all my future questions because there was no one who knew what I wanted and what I was capable of better than me! If I wanted the profs in my new classes to know about my Brailler, I had to tell them. If I needed readers to help with extra homework, I had to find them. It was time to start being the captain of my own ship because no one could plot a better course for my life than me.

I decided I would advertise for readers and pay them for their time. I wanted our relationship to have the importance of a business arrangement, not a volunteer opportunity. I discovered very quickly that the reading arrangements I made with female students worked out a lot better on a regular basis than the ones with male students. (Only then did I see Mr. Ogden's wisdom in setting up all female readers for me in high school.)

I think back on my whole adjustment to college as a tough love experience. It didn't mean Notre Dame cared for me any less than OPRF had, it just meant taking care of these things myself was something I'd have to do for the rest of my life, and the time had come to start doing so now!

A NEW FRIEND

One day during those first several weeks of college, I had just left Flanner and was making my way to class with my Brailler, folder of blank paper, and magic markers in one hand and my white cane in the other. Someone who looked like an upperclassman came up and asked me how things were going. For some reason, I didn't answer in my usual "just fine" way, but said something like, "Ha! Not so well. How about you?"

He seemed very interested in my reply and proceeded to ask me a lot of questions about my white cane, my Brailler, and my eyesight in general. By the end of our short walk together, he had offered to help me read anything I needed help with, and I discovered he not only lived on my floor in Flanner but was not an upperclassman, like I'd suspected, but a lowly freshman just like myself. This was the first time I met Joe Camarda, and he was already on his way to becoming not only my roommate for the next three years, but my best friend at Notre Dame.

Years later, Joe says one of the luckiest moments in his life came a short time after this when he and I, as well as my dad, had a bit of a showdown over whether or not Joe would be paid for the reading he wanted to do for me. "The day I said, 'I do it for free or I don't do it' was a good day because that was the first bond of my most important college relationship," says Joe. "I often think about that."

Joe was not only friendly and outgoing, he was adventurous and just the kind of guy I wanted to hang out and experience college with. He even ended up being my unofficial college career counselor! Near the end of our freshman year, Joe asked me what I was going to declare as my major. Trying to be pragmatic and realistic, I said I had only heard of visually impaired people being teachers or lawyers, so I thought I was going to stay in General Program as my major. "What? Are you nuts?!" Joe exclaimed. "Business is where all the jobs are, and that's where there's money to be made!" I thought about it for about two seconds and then agreed, "Yeah, I'll do business!"

It turned out to have been the perfect choice. After getting a taste of accounting, marketing, management, and finance, I was drawn to finance. I remembered back about ten years earlier when I had taken my little passbook into the bank to have the interest compounded. When the teller handed me the passbook back, I had received $1.86 in interest for doing absolutely nothing! At that time, Pete and I were doing chores around the house like cutting the grass and shoveling the sidewalk for a weekly allowance of 50 cents. And now the bank was going to give me three times that amount for doing nothing but letting them hold my money? I was all over that! I became a saver for the rest of my life. And now I was going to learn how to do that even better, as well as eventually find my way to a job where I told others how to save and invest their money.

Joe and I became roommates during sophomore year. Pete stayed in Morrissey Hall, but all three of us hung together and explored the things Notre Dame and college life had to offer.

For junior year, Pete and all his fellow archie classmates moved to the Notre Dame Architecture Program in Rome, Italy, for their classes. Joe and I stayed on the Notre Dame campus as roommates for another year. As a side note, at Christmastime that year, my parents let me take another huge step in my quest for self-confidence and independence. I boarded a jetliner and flew to Rome to spend Christmas break with Pete and his archie friends, traveling around Europe. As has happened so many times over the years, people reached out and helped me in lots of small ways, and I now see God's love for me in every experience.

With Pete away, I was even more thankful to have Joe as my roommate at Notre Dame. When we returned to campus that fall, I discovered another wonderful thing Joe had done for me. Joe read a lot of books for pleasure, and he'd read one over the summer he knew I would like. So before he came back to Notre Dame, he sat down and recorded the whole thing on cassette tapes. The book was *Marathon Man*, and it will always be my most favorite recorded book I ever read because the voice of the reader was my best friend.

"You were always kind and thoughtful—full of substance if a little light on self confidence," says Joe of me in college. "I never was too thoughtful and had no substance, but I had way, way, way, too much self confidence. We were a very good Punch and Judy, and we made each other better."

Most of my friends in high school had known me before my vision loss, so they knew that I was really just a regular guy. But like Joe, all the friends I would make for the rest of my life would know me only with my visual impairment. I suspected that the first thing people saw about me now was my visual impairment, and most weren't quite sure what to say or do about it. Having the white cane was a lot like being in a wheelchair—I wished I didn't need it, but it absolutely had to be there for most situations!

I tried to use my white cane in only the most necessary circumstances, like crossing a street by myself. In most social settings, I folded it up as quickly as I could and put it out of sight. But as my general level of confidence grew, and I found myself in more and more unfamiliar places, my white cane became an indispensable tool for my own independence. One particular scenario occurred time after time: I would be at a familiar restaurant or bar and need to go to the bathroom. I would walk without my cane to the place where the bathroom was, only to find two different doors. Of course, one of these was the men's room and the other was the ladies' room.

Unable to tell which one was which, I would ask the next passersby if the first door was the men's room. I could not see the expression on their faces, but I could always hear a slight hesitation in the answers, as if they were expecting me to tell them they were on *Candid Camera* or something. Their answers would always be something like, "Yeah, this door with the big sign saying men's room is indeed the men's room." Realizing how stupid the question must have sounded, I would then launch into some long explanation of my impaired vision. Eventually I realized having the white cane did all my explaining for me!

At one point, I realized that being visually impaired was like being four feet tall: I might not like it, but the sooner I accepted it, the sooner I could get on with using all my energy to live my life, rather than moaning about this or that. I also realized that no one could pity me if I did not pity myself. So over the years, my attitude about my cane has shifted to regarding it as essential to going out, just like my wallet or keys or watch.

It's also clear to me now that Joe engaged me in that first conversation because he was curious about the guy he saw walking with a white cane and Braille writing machine. I'm sure I would have come to know who Joe Camarda was during my four years at Notre Dame, but we would not have been drawn so closely together so early if not for my blindness. I believe God used my impaired vision to bring Joe into my life.

I soon realized that just as with my professors, I would have to be the one to show and tell the new people in my life what I wanted them to know about me. This is why my life has become more adventurous since my sight loss, not less!

MOVING FORWARD

My time at Notre Dame went by quickly. There were classes during the day, and then there was reading and homework at night. Listening to all my books on tape, or having my readers read them to me, took at least an extra couple of hours a night. This extra demand on my time seriously cut into what was available for drinking and carousing, but that probably was not a bad thing in retrospect!

In 1978 I graduated from Notre Dame with a bachelor's degree in business administration. In addition to that diploma, Notre Dame is also the origin of one of my most favorite bits of wisdom. Lou Holtz was Notre Dame's head football coach several years after Pete and I graduated. He retired from coaching in 1996, and I did something I have never done before or since: I wrote him a letter to wish him well in whatever he did next. To my utter amazement, he wrote me a short note back that said, "I don't know what the future holds, but I know who holds the future." I have called upon these words of wisdom for support many times since my days at Notre Dame.

GRADUATE SCHOOL

Following my graduation from Notre Dame, I moved to Evanston, Illinois, to attend Northwestern University's Graduate School of Management and get my MBA. This was not any kind of master plan on my part, it was simply the alternative to doing nothing. I had been unable to find a job, despite many job interviews while at Notre Dame.

Northwestern had a unique MBA program that allowed you to receive your master's degree in just four quarters, rather than the usual six. It also meant I had to start the program just weeks after graduating from Notre Dame. There were about 70 students in the program, and classes were intense and moved quickly. My roommate there was Dave Gimbert, or Boots as we came to call him. He was fun and adventurous and just what I was looking for!

Dave was very easygoing on the outside, but he wanted to be where the action was. He was quick to make friends with the other four-quarter students, and he was always asking where people were going and what they were doing.

Many of us in the four-quarter program had come right from undergraduate programs, so being at Northwestern was sort of a second senior year. My classmates were some of the most high-powered and intelligent people I have ever known, and I was surprised to find that practically all of them were also some of the nicest and friendliest people I have ever known. Part of me wanted to make up for lost time and have all the fun I should have had at Notre Dame. Because we were practically the only people on the Northwestern campus during that first summer quarter, our class did almost everything together—including having fun at night and on the weekends.

During one of our parties that first summer, I found myself dancing with the most beautiful girl I had ever met. Her name was Carol. How did I know she was beautiful? Well, she was fun and exciting, and her long hair was blond, of course. She was the perfect height: just a little shorter than me. Her face may have been a blur, especially that first night, but she was gorgeous to me. And for anyone, whether your vision is 20/20 or not, that's what matters.

In college I'd realized that our society (and maybe guys in particular) can get hung up on meaningless physical imperfections. One time some guys had corrected me after I'd said a woman was cute because they said she had a "complexion problem." I thought to myself that it might not be so bad if everyone's eyesight was like mine. We'd all be less judgmental about appearances. Although, for the record, no one ever corrected me about Carol.

I had not really done any dating during my undergraduate years, primarily because keeping up with classes was so challenging, but there was also the fact that all the girls seemed a lot smarter than me, and there were certainly lots of more attractive men than me for them to choose from. As I saw it, this was not poor self esteem on my part, just a realistic evaluation of the situation at hand and an attempt to manage my own expectations.

But now, here I was in graduate school, and the girls were even smarter, and there was even stronger male competition. Yet I was having a great time with this beautiful girl. How could that be? When we finished our song, Carol said I was a good dancer. I told her I liked to dance a lot, but I didn't think I was very good, and I sure would like to take lessons someday. Carol said there was a place giving dance lessons right here at the university, and she wanted to take lessons too. We agreed in an instant that we would take the lessons together! This was 1978, and the lessons we took were for disco dancing. I really enjoyed it, and I think she did too.

ON THE DANCE FLOOR

I suspect that our dance class experience was similar to most others: all the students stood at one end of the dance floor while the male and female teachers demonstrated the dance moves at the other end. Just like learning to ski, I had to make adjustments because I could not see any dance moves beyond six feet away. I explained my situation to the teachers and moved to within about three feet of them to watch their teaching.

Even then, many of the moves weren't exactly what I thought they were, which sometimes lead Carol and I to dissolve into a tangle of arms and legs as we tried to move fluidly across the dance floor. That lead to a litany of "I'm sorry! I'm sorry!" from both of us. Finally, we agreed that there would always be two fundamental rules while dancing: don't ever let go of your partner, (because the visually impaired partner can't find you if you do) and "Dancing means never having to say you're sorry." (Take that, Ryan O'Neal!) We did concede that oops was acceptable and would count as a mild admission of guilt for a dance faux pas. Even today I advise all my dance partners of these precepts.

The key to really getting good on the dance floor is practicing over and over, hopefully with the same partner. And the man has to know how to lead! As a polite, well-mannered man, I had always tried to dance while constantly looking to my partner to see what she wanted to do next, and then trying to do it. I came to realize that this was as disastrous as trying to drive a car while looking for your passenger to make the next turn!

I have no doubt that the skills I learned in that dance class with Carol have been used more in the last 30 years than anything else I learned in class at Notre Dame or Northwestern! Not only have I done lots of dancing since those days and used what I learned on the dance floor, but I also apply them generally and don't apologize for every slip-up in my life!

ANOTHER NEW FRIEND

After our dance experience, Carol knew I was in need of readers for some of our class material, and she volunteered to do that too. This began with her doing reading for me, but the more time we spent together, the less time we spent reading, until we weren't doing any of that at all.

Carol was my best friend at Northwestern. She was a great help with the classes, and our dancing together was some of the best times I've ever had. When I think back on all the good times at Northwestern, Carol is always in those memories.

During our third quarter at Northwestern, the dean of the MBA program made a dramatic announcement. During a special assembly he informed us all that the name of the business school was about to change to the Kellogg Graduate School of Management. We had all applied to the Northwestern Graduate School of Management because of its great reputation, and we were all working hard to earn our MBA from that prestigious school. Now the dean was telling us we were not going to receive a diploma from the school we'd applied to, but from a school named after a brand of breakfast cereals. We were disappointed and dismayed, to say the least.

Now, instead of having a great grad school on our resume, we'd be explaining to prospective employers what the heck the Kellogg Graduate School of Management was, and that we'd taken many classes on topics not related to cereal. Jokes were soon rampant that breakfast would be served 24 hours a day in the cafeteria, and Tony the Tiger and the Rice Krispie elves (Snap, Crackle, and Pop) would be featured on our diplomas.

Despite our feelings, the name change happened, and I did what seemed in my best self-interest: I acted like nothing happened. For several years, my resume said I'd graduated from the Northwestern Graduate School of Management, not Kellogg, and I strongly suspect that many of my classmates did the same. Fortunately for us, though, the reputation of Kellogg rose quickly, and I eventually adjusted my resume for full accuracy. Today I am truly proud to be a graduate of the first class of the Kellogg Graduate School of Management.

In fact, during that graduation ceremony, something happened I know I will never forget. As I'd done for both my high school and college graduation ceremonies, I talked with the faculty in advance to be sure I knew exactly how the ceremony was going to happen so I wouldn't have to use my white cane during the big event. I wanted to be positive my eyesight wouldn't cause any embarrassment or accidents.

So, to prepare for my Kellogg graduation, I went to the location where the ceremony would be. I learned I would need to follow another student to a point at the front of the stage and make my way across the stage to receive my diploma. Then I would continue across the rest of the stage to a wall, turn left, find the handrail, and go down four stairs to exit. Seemed like that would work just fine. No need for my white cane to call attention to myself.

On the day of the graduation, the commencement speaker asked everyone to hold their applause until the end of the ceremony. Well, everyone did until it was my turn to cross the stage. As I did, I heard a small burst of applause. *Oh man*, I thought. My parents had already told me how proud they were, but this was obviously my family showing me their support one more time. I appreciated their enthusiasm, but I was embarrassed and a little miffed.

After the whole event was over, my dad asked me how I was feeling about the graduation. I told him I felt great, but I did have to share that I'd been a bit embarrassed to hear the family clapping when I got my diploma. "That wasn't us!" my dad said. "Those were your classmates!" I was speechless for a long time after that.

I've never received another award or recognition that meant more to me than their applause did, and I don't think I ever will.

ৎ৶৵৶

Carol and I dated throughout graduate school and for some time after that. Soon after we both graduated and found jobs, it was the natural time to think about getting married. But I realized I was not ready for such a commitment. All that time with Carol gave me a glimpse of how wonderful it was to have a serious relationship with another person, and I had never enjoyed something as much before. But, sadly, all that would have to wait for now. I was not secure at all in the career that lay ahead of me, or in my ability to sustain such an important personal relationship.

I believe God put Carol in my life during my time at Kellogg to be my friend and assist me with my many challenges there, but also to show me how wonderful the next stage of my life would be. I'm so thankful for her friendship and all she shared with me.

ADULTHOOD

BREAKING INTO THE REAL WORLD OF WORK

Near the end of my year at Kellogg, it was again time to interview for jobs. I now had both an undergraduate and graduate degree related to finance, so I interviewed with any company that appeared to have anything to do with the industry. Ultimately, I had no idea if I would be successful at getting a job because of my vision. So I deliberately set the bar of expectations very low. My objective was to find a job—any job—that would pay me enough to live independently. I knew I was a prudent spender and very good saver, so I was not bothered by expectations for advancement or apprehensive that I would not enjoy the job. I was getting a job to make money to live, not to enjoy myself! Enjoying myself was what I hoped to do when the work day was over. If I found a paying job that I also enjoyed, that would be pure gravy.

For one of my many interviews, I talked with a municipal bond salesman from the John Nuveen company. At the end of our interview, he said he thought I was smart and a very nice guy, but he didn't know how I would ever do this job with my limited eyesight. He recommended that I contact a man named Don Bonniwell.

Don Bonniwell had been in the municipal bond industry for many years and had become blind later in life. He had continued to work in the municipal bond industry and had become quite a success. All his friends called him "Bonny."

Wow! Finally here was someone with a visual impairment who had seemingly succeeded in find a great job that could be done despite his eyesight. I definitely wanted to meet him and find out how he had accomplished so much in the "sighted world."

I got Mr. Bonniwell's telephone number and called him soon after that interview. We met, and he gave me some great advice. He recommended that I look for a job in the municipal bond industry because "munis" were bought and sold "over the counter." This meant transactions were done over the phone and not through some electronic exchange, so there were no screens or tapes to watch, and my bad eyesight was not a negative. He also recommended that I steer my job search to companies on the "buy side" of the muni bond market, or those that bought municipal bonds—like bank trust departments, insurance companies, and mutual funds—rather than applying to large investment companies looking for salesmen to sell stocks and bonds. This way, I could be in a position where salesmen would do all the watching and searching for bonds I wanted to buy.

I took Bonny's advice and soon had an interview with the trust department at the First National Bank of Chicago. I know Bonny had a lot to do with me getting my first job there, as he had a strong relationship with that institution. My job there was simply a matter of talking to municipal bond salesmen on the phone and making decisions on which bonds to buy.

I had stumbled across the perfect industry

for me. In retrospect, I realize God put Bonny and the bond salesman from John Nuveen in my life at just the right time, and I am so thankful. It was God who led me to that job.

THE "MUNI GO-FOR"

However, my first couple of years at the bank were more tough love, not at all easy or touchy feely. My job was to sit behind the municipal bond trading desk and pretty much do anything anyone else needed and did not want to do themselves. This made me the "Muni Go-For," but despite the challenges, I did not mind this one bit. I was so pleased to have a job and be learning about a whole industry I knew nothing about.

Dressing appropriately for my position was not something anyone talked to me about, and I started in the middle of August, when Chicago weather was at its hottest. To prepare, I had gone to your basic suit store and purchased two new suits that looked nice to me, one blue and one gray. Both were moderately priced polyester numbers, and I also got some short-sleeve white shirts to go along with them. These seemed to me to be nice additions to the blue, gray, and light brown suits I already had.

Within the first month or two of working, one of my female colleagues obviously took pity on me and quietly told me that if I did not want to be known as the "Prince of Polyester" around the office, I needed to spend some real bucks and buy some nice suits. So I went and did so. Not so long after that, I was walking into the office one day when Glen Wozniak, the head of our money market area, shouted across the room to me, "Hey, elbows, what the heck is with the short-sleeve shirts?" (However, Glenn used much more colorful language than that.) Until then I hadn't known that wearing long-sleeve shirts at the bank was an absolute, no matter what the weather outside was like.

Both these experiences were embarrassing, but I was glad they happened so I could fix the problem. In fact, Glenn would become my best friend at work during those early years. And these were by no means the first embarrassing faux pas that had happened to me, and I knew they wouldn't be the last. So I just kept going.

When I began working in downtown Chicago, Cindy—my old friend and reader from high school—was working there too, and we made a point of getting together for lunch a couple times a year on Michigan Avenue. After a number of years in Chicago, Cindy moved to Florida where her mother had moved a couple years earlier.

A few years ago, I got a call from one of Cindy's cousins, who also happened to be a high school classmate of mine. She let me know that Cindy had passed away several months earlier from a complication of her diabetes. Since then her family had been trying to think of all the people they needed to contact, and they thought of me. Today, every time I walk up Michigan Avenue I think of Cindy and what a blessing she was to my life. I wish we were having lunch again, and I wish I could thank her just one more time for all she did and what she meant to me.

As the months and years of working at the bank went by, I perfected what I called the Lotto Ball Theory of Promotion. If I just kept working hard in my spot, eventually the people above me would move on, and I would get sucked up to their positions. Following this theory, I moved from analyst to bond trader to fund manager. (Personal note: The Lotto Ball Theory of Promotion worked for me, but I do not recommend it for others. This method takes a very long time, and a talented employee with a good work ethic can do much better following a more intentional career-development path!)

I worked for First Chicago for 17 years. My career was very successful and fulfilling, and I had a number of great successes in my job there, and some failures too—but I had more of the first than the second! Based on that, I look back fondly on my time at First Chicago.

STEP THREE OF MY SPIRITUAL JOURNEY

A year or so after I started working at First Chicago, I got a call from Beth, who was a friend of Jules Mason, the wife of my best high school friend, Dick Mason. Beth and I had met at Dick and Jules' wedding just a few months earlier. Now she was calling to invite me to go with her to a singles' Bible study up on the north side of Chicago called The Hub. I accepted immediately, but it wasn't because I was interested in any kind of Bible study—it was because Beth was very attractive and she was a blonde!

The Hub met in the early evening at the Salvation Army office near Wrigley Field. The program consisted of an opening with music and then a lesson taught by a guest speaker.

I enjoyed that first visit very much, but I realized The Hub was just too far away from home for me to attend on a regular basis. I would be taking public transportation for well over two hours round trip each time I came. Also, I realized Beth's intentions were simply to introduce me to The Hub. She didn't have any romantic interest in me at all.

But before the meeting was over, another girl came up and introduced herself as Judy. She said she and I had been classmates during high school, and she remembered me from Mr. McGintey's creative writing class. But she said she didn't expect me to remember her because she'd been a very quiet person during high school. Judy said she lived in Oak Park now, where I was living, and would be willing to give me a ride to The Hub anytime I wanted.

The very next week, Judy called and offered to drive me to The Hub that night if I was going. I took her up on the offer. In no time, Judy and I were going to The Hub on a regular basis. One of the first lessons I heard was a study of the book of Romans. As the lesson progressed, I felt as though the teacher somehow knew about my episode in Colorado at the Young Life camp, because he proceeded to methodically address the list of conflicts that had arisen that night six years earlier.

First, The Hub speaker went to Romans 3:23: "For all have sinned and fall short of the glory of God." No one, no one at all is good enough to earn their way into heaven. Original sin, or simply human nature, totally stops us from ever being able to earn our way into heaven. Trying to "be good" just to earn your way into heaven was a waste of time and missed the point of God's incredible love, shared through Jesus Christ.

Then he went to Ephesians 2:8, 9: "For it is by grace you have been saved, through faith, and this is not from yourselves. It is the gift of God, not by works, so no one can boast." God's grace, the gift of Jesus as a sacrifice for all sins, is what opens heaven to mankind, not any list of good works we do ourselves.

This is what explains both the parables of the prodigal son and the workers in the field. I think both of them are actually misnamed. Their titles should be "The Father of the Prodigal Son," and "The Owner of the Field," because the parables are about God, not about the son or the workers. The work or good things we do here on earth by themselves do not add up to a ticket to heaven.

We do whatever we can here just because God loves us so much, and we love Him back. Jesus says, "Whoever has my commands and obeys them, he is the one who loves Me. Whoever loves me will be loved by my Father, and I too will love him and show myself to him." John 14:21

Now maybe that's not how you or I would set things up, but God's ways aren't our ways! And as far as why Jesus had to come into the world, He did much more than just teach us about loving each other. He came to pay for our sins because God is both all love and all justice too. No one ever has to worry about anyone else getting away with something or not following the rules as well as they are.

And, as far as my objection that salvation seemed too easy, the speaker pointed out that there was nothing easy about Jesus dying on the cross. It was truly a painful and horrific death that showed not only the consequences of sin, but the incredible magnitude of God's love for us and His willingness to pay the penalty for our sins. "For God so loved the world that He gave His only son, that we may have eternal life." John 3:16

So, if you believe that Jesus is the Son of God (and I did), and you are truly sorry for your sins (and I was), then not to believe salvation is assured through Jesus's death and resurrection is to be at the foot of the cross either saying, "Nice gesture, Jesus, but that's not enough for me." or "No thanks, Jesus. I want to get to heaven on my own good works." I wasn't going to say either of those things. *Wow!* I thought. *It finally all makes sense, and it all fits together.* I felt like I'd just put together the answer to the world's greatest murder mystery! I wondered what else I could learn if I read more of the Bible and came back to The Hub.

So I did keep coming back, and I felt more and more a part of the program. Coming early to The Hub and helping to move chairs became very much a part of my participation. I knew I wasn't familiar enough with scripture to help with any of the teaching, but I was very good at moving tables and chairs.

During one of my early visits to The Hub,

a leader asked if I would open the evening with prayer. I said, "No, I'm sure there are much more qualified people around to open in prayer." The leader said fine and moved on, but I felt so guilty about not being able to open a meeting with a simple prayer that I started to listen carefully to others who prayed. I started piecing together a prayer of my own. Not long afterward, I volunteered to open the meeting in prayer and successfully did so.

Sometime later, I came across the scripture passage that would come to be my very favorite: John 9:1-3. It's the story of Jesus and His disciples coming across a blind man. The disciples ask Jesus if the man was blind because of his own sins or the sins of his father as the Old Testament said. Jesus answered them, "Neither this man nor his parents sinned but this happened so that the work of God might be displayed in his life." Then Jesus proceeds to heal the blind man.

Wow, there it was: the explanation for the loss of my sight. God had done amazing things in my life, but I needed to have the experience of losing my sight to see that! Also, I was beginning to see that God had many, many more blessings in store for me, and my sight loss was necessary for those things to happen. If God is love, then God's work is love, and if the blind man in the parable lost his sight so that the work of God might be displayed, then it truly made sense to me that that's why I lost my sight too.

Today, what scripture says about God's plan for each of us seems a lot clearer to me and not so filled with contradictions as it did many years ago. It's amazing how God brought me to The Hub and how He used both Beth and Judy to keep me there long enough to learn what I needed to know—that God's ways are not man's ways. Where I got confused was trying to fit God and Jesus into the precepts I had come to accept from society and the manmade rules around me.

The Hub also introduced me to an idea I had not heard of before: the idea that each of us should look for a mate who is "equally yoked" to God, or rather, someone at a similar place in his or her faith (2 Corinthians 6:14).

As I saw it, this was an additional hurdle to finding the girl who would become my wife. It wasn't like I had the luxury of being able to narrow the universe of eligible spouse candidates. My life was not some kind of Hai Karate aftershave commercial where I was fighting off women! Reluctantly, though, I decided I would keep the idea in mind and see how it went.

I was eventually asked to be on the Board of The Hub. Just like when that leader asked me to open the meeting in prayer, I told them I felt there were far more qualified people, but if they really felt I could add something, I would be honored to serve. I did so for a good five years.

THE DATING LIFE

For the next several years, my work kept me very busy. I was getting more and more responsibility and jobs to do as others in my department left to take new opportunities. I often stayed a little after work to clean up loose ends and prepare for the next day.

In the midst of all that, making arrangements to meet and set dates with women was proving to be a difficult task. As I had discovered in high school, I could not spot a girl at a distance and decide whether she was the type I was going to go after. (I heard stories of guys doing this all the time!) Conversely, because I couldn't see them, I couldn't respond to any girl who might spot me and try to drop some kind of visual sign that she was interested, like a wink or a smile.

I know for a fact that one such event happened. A young woman who worked in another area of the bank met me at several municipal bond functions, where I was not using my white cane. She knew I was a nice guy, and I assume she thought I was okay looking, so she would smile and wave at me when our paths crossed in the lobby or cafeteria of the bank, and other times when I was not using my white cane. Of course, I did not see her, so I appeared to ignore her totally.

One day, she shared with another co-worker these experiences and her frustration that I was "acting like such a jerk by ignoring her." The co-worker, who knew me better, laughed and exclaimed, "You idiot, don't you know he's legally blind? He can't see you!"

Luckily, she had a great sense of humor and was the type of person who eventually felt comfortable enough to share the story with me. Last I heard, she's married and lives in Florida.

With challenges like this, I had to focus on opportunities where I was thrown together with available women. This led to a little remorse that I hadn't made better use of the opportunity Notre Dame had offered to meet girls. And if you are narrowing the universe of candidates to those who are only Christians, the task gets even harder! Nevertheless, after later analysis, I can say that the Bible is true: all things work for the good for those who believe (Romans 8:28).

Very early in 1984, the American Blind Skiing Foundation began annual trips to well-known ski resorts, and one of the first they chose was Banff, Canada! This sounded like an exotic destination and a trip of a lifetime, so I signed up immediately.

When the trip came along in March, we stayed at beautiful accommodations—The Banff Springs Hotel—and had the unique opportunity to meet up with a group of Canadian visually impaired skiers who happened to be there at the same time. We had a sort of pizza dinner together and then hung around and played board games, like Trivial Pursuit. When the game playing began, I was captivated by one of the Canadian skiers.

Her name was Brenda, and her fun, friendly, and confident personality drew me like a magnet. A short time later, we found ourselves dancing. Soon after we started, she said to me in a very matter-of-fact tone, "Oh, it's so refreshing to dance with a man who knows how to lead." Well, no one had complimented me like that in a very long time, so this girl was building up all kinds of great marks in my book! But, it was the next thing she said that knocked my socks off.

"You're a Christian, aren't you?" she added.

I think I stammered something like, "Uh, yeah, but how did you know that?"

"Oh, it shows," she said.

Well, that may have been the greatest compliment I had ever received, and I had to know more about this woman. When we finished dancing, I asked her where she was going to be skiing the next day because I wanted to meet her for lunch, coffee—any reason I could think of!

"Our group is leaving in the morning," she said, and my heart sank.

NO!!! a silent voice inside me shouted. So I talked her into meeting me for breakfast before they left. She brought a friend with her, so I did not share all the feelings I had experienced the night before. But I began making plans to visit

Brenda as soon as I returned to Chicago, and I soon flew to Edmonton, Alberta, to see her. I thought the visit went well, but I played it cool again because I had an enormous fear the whole visit that I might come on too strong and scare her away. After all, she was a graduate student finishing up her studies, and I was just this foreign guy she had met on a ski trip!

A short time after that visit, Brenda wrote and told me she just wanted to be friends. I was stunned. I couldn't make any sense of the whole thing, because I thought I'd behaved so well! Maybe this plan of mine had backfired… It seemed so obvious to me that God had put her in my life. (And in fact, He did. Brenda is still a good friend of mine today, and I cherish her friendship.)

But then, it dawned on me that God had taken me 1,600 miles away from home to show me He knew what I was looking for in a partner and that He could introduce me to someone as great as Brenda. And if He could do that, He could and would certainly find such a person for me in Chicago! He would have one for me when the time was right. I just had to trust in Him. So I gave up the idea of finding my own mate and put the job in God's hands. He came through for me sooner than I ever expected.

A NEW BEST FRIEND, FOR THE REST OF MY LIFE

In the summer of 1984, I received a save the date announcement for my 10-year high school reunion coming up in the fall. I had attended a grade-school reunion several years earlier and had a great time, so I decided I would go to the high school reunion too. But I didn't think about it much after that. The prospects of meeting someone there who was new and exciting, and a Christian to boot, seemed slim to none.

A month or two before the reunion, I was talking with a high school classmate of mine, Al Peyton. Al and his wife, Liz, lived in Oak Park and were going to the reunion too. Al asked me if I already had a date and said he and Liz knew a girl from church they wanted to introduce me to. He thought the reunion would be a great opportunity for us to have a first date. Al was not known as a matchmaker, so I suspect this was Liz's idea, but I was grateful for the thought. However, I told Al the whole plan was dumb. If I went to the reunion and had a good time with my old classmates, this girl might feel left out. Plus, this was the first time I was going to see many of these people in 10 years—I couldn't show up with just anyone as my date!

But Al was persistent. He said maybe all four of us could have a quick double date before the reunion so I could check this girl out. I decided that was not a bad idea. Her name was Jane Hatfield, and I took down her phone number to call her. She was from Camp Hill, Pennsylvania, a suburb of Harrisburg. She had come to Chicago to go to Wheaton College, where her Mom had gone to college too. Jane and I had graduated from college the same year, and she'd taken a job as a banker at American National Bank right after school. (I was attending Kellogg at that time.) Jane lived in Wheaton for a short time after college, but she moved to Oak Park for a better commute downtown. Now she lived only three blocks away from me. That's what I call geographically desirable!

But Al beat me to the punch. He immediately called Jane after he and I talked and told her a friend of his would be calling her soon to ask her out. He went on to say that this friend lived in Oak Park, was a banker just like she was, was a graduate of Notre Dame and Kellogg, plus any other factoids he could think of that put me in a positive light.

Then he asked Jane, "You would go out on a date with a guy like that, right?"

She said, "Well, sure, I guess."

Then Al said, "Great! Liz and I are looking forward to it. Oh yeah, one last thing, my friend is blind. That's okay, right?"

Jane remembers thinking to herself, Oh great, now what do I say? So she said, "Oh, no problem. That's just fine."

As she hung up the phone, her roommate asked, "What was that all about?"

"I'm going on a blind date," Jane said. "No, I mean I'm going out with a date who's blind!" Then she sat back and waited to hear from this mysterious blind guy.

When I finally got around to calling Jane, I asked her if she wanted to go to the movies on a double date with Al and Liz. There was a movie theater just a block away from where we lived, and I recommended we all meet right there. Jane said that would be just fine, but she does remember thinking it was strange that a blind guy wanted to go to the movies!

Following my usual movie viewing policy, Jane and I sat in the fifth row of the theater, then went back to my apartment for pizza with Liz and Al. When the date was over, I thought things had gone very well. Jane was really cute, friendly, smart, laughed at my jokes, and, yes, she was blond! So I took the next step and asked her to come to the reunion with me. Jane already knew that several other friends of hers would be at the reunion, so she said yes to that too.

The reunion was lots of fun. Not only did I enjoy being with Jane, but I saw lots of old friends and former classmates. At the time, I thought I did a really nice job of balancing the reunion night between spending time with Jane and catching up with my old classmates. However, to this day, Jane likes to pull my chain when we talk about the reunion. She tells people she didn't mind at all when girls kept coming up to her and saying, "You came with John Erickson. Do you know where he is?"

Now let me say I wasn't totally clueless about what a nice thing it was that Jane put up with going to the reunion! Whether or not she and I were meant to be, I knew at the least I owed her some nice dinners out and the like—that is, if she would ever go out with me again! But she did. We spent more and more time together in the weeks and months after the reunion.

About three months after the reunion, I had plans to spend my two weeks of vacation doing some skiing in Colorado, then going to visit my old friend Betsy Kettlehut (from our summers at the cottage in Michigan), now Betsy Koepsel, and her husband, Ron. They had just moved to Boca Raton, Florida, from Chicago the prior year.

I found out that Jane had plans to visit her grandfather in Boca Raton, and our trips overlapped one weekend. So Betsy, Ron, and I picked up Jane at her grandfather's house and spent two nights seeing the sights in Boca. We had a great time, and then Jane left to go back to Chicago.

That evening, Betsy told me she thought Jane was great and I should call and ask her to come back down to Boca the next weekend. I explained to Betsy that I thought that was a nice idea, but I already knew Jane was the kind of woman who was orderly and made her plans long in advance. It was doubtful she would just pick up and travel to Boca Raton on a minute's notice. Betsy said, "Fine. Call her and check." So I called Jane and invited her to come back down. Much to my surprise, she said she would check the airfares and call me back.

The next day, Jane called to say she had checked the flights back to Florida, and the only tickets available were first class. She thought the prices were way too high to warrant a trip back. When I conveyed this message to Betsy, she simply said, "Give Jane your credit card." Much to my surprise, Jane took the card number over the phone and said she would book the flight!

Jane flew back that next weekend, and we had another fun time with Ron and Betsy. That little spontaneous excursion to Florida told me a lot about Jane I didn't know, and I liked it all! And I'm sure it told Jane a lot about me too.

Over the next nine months or so, Jane and I did lots of things together. For a while, we called each other every morning and did our daily devotions together. She met the rest of my family, and we flew to Harrisburg and I met hers too. Our offices in downtown Chicago were only three blocks apart, so we did our best to schedule lunches here and there. But both of us were very dedicated to our jobs, so we spent most of our time together after work.

I don't remember ever having any big discussions about my eyesight. What I loved so much about being with Jane was her never-ending positive attitude about life and her apparent enjoyment of being with me. I don't remember any awkward times of trying to figure out what she meant by a comment. She was so genuine. And her care for people was apparent.

When the fall came, the light bulb in my head went on, and I realized Jane was the lifetime mate I was looking for. God had found her and put her in my life. At Thanksgiving, we visited Jane's parents, and I asked her dad for his blessing to marry her. Then it was time to decide when I was going to pop the question. Christmas and New Years seemed too obvious, and Super Bowl Sunday wasn't on the same day each year, so I chose Groundhog Day. By picking a secondary holiday as the date of our engagement, I thought I would elevate our future enjoyment of that day, as well as give me an easy tool to help remember the date.

That night, there was a James Bond movie on TV, so inviting Jane over for the evening was not suspicious. During a commercial, I turned the volume down and told her I had a Groundhog Day present for her. She unwrapped a medium-size box to find a small toy squirrel with a note in his hand. (Finding a groundhog stuffed animal was not as easy as I thought it would be!) The note said, "My cousin the groundhog is very busy today, so I am delivering this message for him. John Erickson wants to marry you, and he wants to know if you will marry him! You can give him your answer directly."

Jane quietly read this note to herself, and I was delighted and relieved when she turned to me with a big smile and said yes.

Jane and I got married in 1986 in Harrisburg, PA, at Jane's childhood church. Our faith in God is stronger and deeper because we married each other, and there are two things about our wedding I'll always remember: one, just a couple days before I left Chicago for the wedding, I cracked a small bone in my toe. By the morning of the wedding, my foot didn't hurt at all, but it had swollen so much that I couldn't fit into my tuxedo shoes. My dad came through for me again, as I ended up wearing his shoes for the wedding.

Second, as the ceremony began, I waited at the front of the church with my groomsmen. The music began playing as the bridal party came down the main aisle. All the bridesmaids made their way to the front of the church, but there was no Jane following them. The music just kept playing, and I kept waiting for Jane to appear through the fog of my poor eyesight. I found out later she was three-quarters of the way down the aisle, just out of my vision range, waiting for the photographer to reload his camera with film, but all that time I stood at the front of the church and wondered if she had changed her mind about marrying me.

FAMILY MAN

As we began our life together, although we were both bankers by career, we agreed that I would be the one responsible for saving and budgeting, while Jane would handle the day-to-day finances, as well as our social calendar. We both do our best to keep the other informed about our duties, and we have found that when one of us is depressed or down about something, the other can be uplifting and a reminder of how blessed our lives are.

Jane is outstanding at reading people and determining their concerns and needs, and I am not. We work well as complements to each other, which makes our match a great one. And when we've faced what appear to be irreconcilable differences, we pray about it and try to put any resolution in God's hands.

Our son, JP, was born in 1988, just over two years after we were married, and our daughter, Ellie, was born two and a half years later in 1991. I never could have imagined how wonderful it would be to be a father and bring up a family. Now that I know how much love I have for a child, I realize the true depth of God's love for His children defies our understanding. And I know that He loves me.

When the kids were little we tried to address my "bad eyesight" directly. As they got a little older, I even tried to put a positive spin on my eyesight. I offered to speak to different grade school classes about being visually impaired, and I showed and demonstrated my cool aids and appliances for students.

When JP was about six, Jane asked him what kind of car he was going to buy when he grew up. He answered dead seriously. He said he was not going to drive when he grew up. He was going to have Allison (one of his friends) drive all the time, just like Jane did for me. Jane did her best to explain why that idea was probably not going to fly.

༄༅༄༅

This was about 1996, and it appeared to me that all systems were go for our lives ahead. My job was going great. I was running municipal bond funds now and receiving awards from Lipper Analytical Service and The American Banking Association for top performing funds in their category. We had just moved to a bigger house in River Forest, and the kids were enjoying school there. Then, out of the blue, just as I started to feel comfortable with the idea of working at one place my whole career, First Chicago merged with NBD Bank in Detroit. They moved the investment trading unit of the wealth management department to Detroit. I was invited to come, but Jane and I decided our lives were in Chicago now, and this was where we were going to stay.

So I had to face the unthinkable: voluntarily giving up my job that I loved so much and finding a new one. Although this went against my whole essence, I saw the big picture for one of the first times, and I knew leaving the bank to stay in Chicago was the right thing to do. Fortunately, the bank had a fantastic severance program, which rewarded those like me who had stuck it out for so many years.

While I wasn't working, most weekdays I got up and went to the bank's outplacement office to research and find other job opportunities, but also did every personal summer activity I wanted to. This included being a Little League coach for JP's team, which was a great way to relive my great memories of being in Little League so many years ago.

After four months of having great fun and still looking for that next job, I called one of my old colleagues at First Chicago, Jeff Roberts, to ask a question. When we spoke, he said he thought I'd found another job months ago. When I told him I hadn't, he got back to me with a job offer as an account manager within the wealth management department, and I was delighted! Although the investment unit that traded securities had moved to Detroit, the people who had personal contact with clients had not, and now I was going to be a part of that group.

I returned to First Chicago for about eight months, but then I received a phone call from Mark Quinn, my former boss at the bank who had also been let go. Mark told me he had just finished an interview at LaSalle Bank, and they were specifically looking for someone with a lot of municipal bond experience. He told me I needed to give LaSalle a call because he thought I was the perfect person for that job.

Well, Mark was right. I spoke with LaSalle and they hired me as the director of fixed income within the wealth management department. I worked for LaSalle for the next twelve years. Just like my time at First Chicago, I had many great successes at LaSalle, and a couple big blunders too, but there were many more of the first than the second, so I look back on my time at LaSalle fondly.

※ ※ ※ ※

When JP was in high school, I found myself behind the wheel of a car for the first time since I'd crashed into the house in high school while trying to back out of the garage. I was in a big parking lot helping JP in a capacity few other parents could. He had a high school project about the feasibility of a car a blind person could drive. The car would have outward-pointing sensors that would report to the blind driver. Four of JP's friends were in he car with us, and each was acting like one of the outward sensors. As I tried to pull in and out of parking places based on the audio input of my human sensors, JP suddenly announced, "Dad, pull over! There's a police car coming up beside us!"

I stopped the car and rolled down my window. "Is there a problem, officer?" I asked casually.

"Well," the policeman said, "you were driving quite erratically back there. Is everything okay?"

"Oh, I'm helping the boys here do a high school project about a car a blind person could drive," I said. The whole time, I was doing my very best to look at the policeman so he would not realize I really was almost blind.

I must have done pretty well because he said, "Okay, fine. Good luck with the project." And he drove away.

⁂

After more than a decade at LaSalle Bank, my career there came to an end when LaSalle was bought by Bank of America. Bank of America had legions of people doing the same thing I was doing, so the elimination of my job in Chicago made sense from their big-picture point of view.

There were not many positions in Chicago like the one I had at LaSalle, so I began thinking about other options. One of those options was to move to a smaller investment advisory firm as a registered investment advisor. In the building right next door to LaSalle Bank, there was such a company, and they invited me to join them after I interviewed there in 2008.

I am still there today, and my responsibilities are primarily to manage the investments of my clients. I love it! I feel like I really have come full circle since that time I was a little kid and I got so excited when my bank gave me interest for the first time. Now I want my clients to be excited about me managing their money!

❧❧❧❧

When I was 50 years old, in 2007, I went with a group of fellas from my church, the First Presbyterian Church of River Forest, out to Park City, Utah, to ski. I called ahead to the ski school at Park City and asked if they had any volunteer guides for the visually impaired. They directed me to the National Ability Center, where I arranged to have a guide ski with me the days I would be there.

The volunteer guide they gave me was Jennifer Gardner. While she and I were skiing, I had the opportunity to tell her the history of my skiing, and at one point I mentioned that I'd tried ski racing when I was in my 20s, but I had bombed! I told her it was my plan to someday to race again and be successful.

"You're in luck," she told me. "There's a race course at the top of this chairlift, and we'll go down that course."

I told her quite emphatically that I hadn't meant right now or today for my return to racing, but she guided me with the perfect balance between encouragement and pushiness. We skied the race course several times that day and walked away with a silver NASTAR (National Standard Racing) medal! NASTAR is a national organization that sets up ski racing competitions at resorts across the country.

Well, now I was hooked on ski racing.

For the next three years, I participated in the NASTAR National Ski Championship and won gold medals, and Jennifer guided me to two of those medals! She is a very special friend today, and we've had opportunities to ski again together several times since that first trip to Park City.

I've had dozens of ski guides over those many years since that first day during my sophomore year in high school. I never would have met any of them if not for my eyesight, and I totally realize that I could never ski on my own—just like the volunteer readers who taped all my textbooks were essential to my academic career. I make it a policy to always buy my ski guide coffee and lunch when we ski together, and I tell them directly how meaningful the skiing—and their help—is to me! Each of them has displayed to me the love God has for me.

GROWING OLDER

In 2007, my son JP graduated from Oak Park-River Forest High School, and Ellie did the same in 2009. JP went on to the University of Iowa and graduated with a degree in cinema. Ellie went to Elon University in North Carolina and graduated with a degree in human services. Both are beginning their own careers now.

And speaking of those who were agents of God's love in my life, my high school buddy Dave is now married and lives in Florida, Kevin lives in Alaska, and Dick is married and lives in Tennessee. My daughter, Ellie, and Dick's daughter, Ginna Claire, are the same age and have known each other since they were infants. Without talking to each other, they both applied to Elon University in North

Carolina and both got in. They put their names into the freshman class lottery for housing and ended up being suite mates. They lived in a house as roommates for the rest of their college time.

My twin brother and first best friend, Pete, is married and has five children. Pete and his family live in Clarendon Hills, just 20 minutes away, and we see each other regularly. My three sisters, Karen, JoAnne, and Mary Christine, are all married and have children too. Karen and Mary Christine both live in Downers Grove with their families, and my sister JoAnne lives in St. Joseph, Michigan—just 25 minutes from our family cottage. My parents, Hub and Joan, are alive and well and live in Downers Grove, Illinois, too, just 30 minutes from Jane and me in River Forest.

✧✧✧✧

Around age 50, another physical challenge came into my life when I began to lose my hearing. The diagnosis came much more quickly this time: premature hearing loss. But there were no treatments or surgeries to fix it.

Long ago I had contemplated the possibility of going totally blind, but the possibility of losing my hearing took me completely by surprise. I was initially very troubled about this new challenge, but slowly I realized that God had supported and strengthened me through every other challenge I'd experienced in my life, and I had faith that this hearing situation would be no different. With the help of hearing aids, that has been the case. The aids have kept me functioning at work, but my conversational skills have suffered, especially in loud or noisy settings.

Nevertheless, throughout my years, God has showed me that I shouldn't put limits on my life or on what I can and cannot do, because that's saying there are limits to what He can accomplish. And there is nothing God can't accomplish.

For this very reason, I have gotten even more adventurous in my old age. Over the last five years, I have twice climbed the stairs of a Chicago high rise in the Hustle Up the Hancock, rappelled three times down 27 stories of the Wit hotel in The Skyline Plunge, and even bungee jumped with JP in Australia!

For my 57th birthday in 2013, Jane saw an ad in the paper for a place called Drive A Tank. She checked out their website and found that visitors could drive a variety of armored vehicles, fire several different belt-fed machine guns, and even crush a real car with a tank. Seeing how our basement is filled with well over a dozen model tanks I've built and painted with the help of my CCTV enlarger, she knew I would love to try that. So she bought me a package for my birthday.

Pete, JP, and I flew to Minneapolis, then drove to Kasota, Minnesota, to the site of Drive A Tank. The experience was beyond my wildest dreams! I would not have even considered putting such a thing on any kind of bucket list, because I couldn't see how it would be possible. However, I told the staff that I was indeed legally blind, and they made it work. I drove a 35-ton self-propelled artillery gun around a path in the woods. One of their staff tapped me on either my left or right shoulder to indicate which way I needed to direct the vehicle. I also used a two-way headset to receive driving instructions.

For the highlight of the day, I climbed into

the driver's seat of a 60-ton British Chieftain main battle tank and proceeded to drive it over the top of a Lincoln Continental.

Later that summer, Jane and I went to California to visit JP, who lives there now for his job. He informed us that he had purchased trapeze lessons for him and me. Of course I thought that was crazy, but I said a prayer and decided I would give it a try. The people at the trapeze school worked with me, and after two hours of practice, I could climb the ladder to the trapeze platform, jump off, swing out, hang by my legs, and finally drop into the net about 20 feet below.

It was yet another God-given opportunity, and He has given me the strength and courage to enjoy them all.

EPILOGUE

It took the loss of my sight for me to see God's love and the true riches of the blessings He has bestowed upon me. My family was the first blessing in my life, and they remain an enormous blessing to me today. I have realized they are one of the first examples of how God turned my seemingly sad physical hardship into something positive and special.

I feel that Jesus has walked beside me all these subsequent years and has shown His love for me by getting me through all the challenges that have arisen. Each of the people who has touched my life has revealed some aspect of God's love to me.

I was recently flying from Tampa to Chicago, and I had a layover of 90 minutes in Atlanta. I went looking for a place to get a sandwich and saw an area with bright lights and what looked like stools with people sitting down. I walked up to a woman there and asked if I could get a sandwich here.

She said, "Sure, you can sit right over here next to me."

I ordered a sandwich, and the waitress soon brought a basket piled high with chips. I figured the sandwich was under the chips, so I started to feel around in the basket for it. The woman who had helped me to the seat saw what I was doing and told me the sandwich was actually on a separate plate behind the basket.

I thanked her for the help and introduced myself. She said her name was Char, and she was going to Pittsburgh on a job interview. Char had been in the real estate business in Florida for 20 years but had just been let go from her job. We shared stories about having had great jobs, and losing them due to circumstances beyond our control. I thought to myself about the last time I had been between jobs and how scary that felt. I've only had to find new work twice in my life, and opportunities popped up pretty quickly. I wondered why God had done that for me, and I prayed to myself that God would find Char a job soon too.

It was then time to catch my plane, so I stood up and thanked Char for her help. "Have a great flight and God bless," I told her.

"God bless you too," Char said.

I nodded and said, "He has."

Made in the USA
San Bernardino, CA
27 April 2014